GIFTED CHILDREN
in the CLASSROOM

Preface

THIS BOOK represents an attempt to highlight some of our newer understandings about the nature of giftedness, the goals of educating gifted children, problems of identification and motivation, and development of giftedness during the preschool years. Since the length of the book is such that it is impossible to present enough to be worthwhile concerning the teaching of gifted children in specific subject areas such as mathematics, science, languages, social studies, art, music, and the like, the choice was made to deal with practical, specific methods and materials which are adaptable for use with all ages and in all areas of the curriculum. It is for this reason that chapters are devoted to the development of creative readers and to the teaching of research concepts and skills.

The final chapter includes a challenge to teachers of gifted children to search for their own unique invention, their way of teaching, and offers some suggestions to speed this search and to facilitate the process of becoming an effective teacher of gifted children.

E. Paul Torrance
University of Minnesota

Contents

GIFTED CHILDREN
in the CLASSROOM

I

Emerging Concepts of Giftedness

MANY TEACHERS, school administrators, counselors, school psychologists, and parents complain that there is no commonly accepted definition of giftedness, even among national and international authorities. When educational and civic leaders plead for support for programs for educating teachers of gifted children or for appropriate educational programs for gifted children, many legislators oppose such support, arguing that not even the experts know how to identify those who are gifted. They contend that if there is disagreement about identifying the gifted it is futile to attempt to educate teachers especially for the gifted and to provide special kinds of educational opportunities for them.

The problem, strangely, is not that the experts do not know how to identify gifted children, nor even that there is any genuine disagreement among the national and international authorities. The truth is that we have been expanding our concept of giftedness and that we have been learning an increasingly large number of ways of identifying a greater number of different kinds of gifted children.

Another problem is that many of those who have sought support for programs for gifted children have had fixed notions about giftedness. In many cases their ideas have been so patently erroneous that their proposals have not made sense to legislators and other would-be supporters. In some cases these fixed ideas have centered around one type of giftedness, usually the type

identified by an intelligence test and represented by the index
known as the "IQ." Until recently there has been little support
for Paul Witty's (1951) definition of giftedness as "consistently
superior performance in any socially useful endeavor." Others
have been overconcerned about the degree of giftedness and
have argued that the gifted must have IQ's of 180, 150, 140, or
some other figure. From arguments around this point there has
arisen a great deal of confusing terminology, such as "genius,"
"highly gifted," "extremely gifted," "moderately gifted," "talented," and the like. Other arguments have centered around the
fixity of the intelligence quotient.

Generally, however, serious students of the problem of educating gifted children agree that our expanding knowledge
makes it clear that the problem is complex but not necessarily
confusing. It is quite clear that there is a variety of kinds of
giftedness that should be cultivated and are not ordinarily cultivated without special efforts. It is clear that if we establish a level
on some single measure of giftedness, we eliminate many extremely gifted individuals on other measures of giftedness. It is
also clear that intelligence may increase or decrease, at least in
terms of available methods of assessing it, depending upon a
variety of physical and psychological factors both within the
individual child and within his environment.

The complexity engendered by our expanding knowledge of
the human mind and its functioning should be exciting and challenging rather than confusing. The author hopes that the reader
will find it so because this is the nature of things as teachers and
parents experience them in trying to educate gifted children.
Furthermore this complex view of the nature of giftedness per-
meates this book. The author hopes that it will help the reader
feel more comfortable, yet excited and challenged, in his efforts
to teach gifted children in elementary and high-school classrooms.

Challenge of a Complex View of Giftedness

The acceptance of a realistically complex view of the human
mind is itself a tremendous advance. In moving from an oversim-
plified (and patently erroneous) view of giftedness to a more

complex one, we have reached a position where we can avoid many of the errors of the past. We should be able to develop a more humane kind of education for gifted children—one in which children will have a better chance to achieve their potentialities.

This more complex view of giftedness is causing us to reevaluate many of the classical experiments upon which we have built educational practices. From this reexamination it is becoming clear that children should be provided opportunities for mastering a variety of learning and thinking skills according to a variety of methods and that the outcomes of these efforts should be evaluated in a variety of ways. It will be one of the purposes of this book to illustrate some of this variety of learning and thinking skills, methods of learning, and evaluation procedures.

It is to hoped that young teachers, as well as experienced educational leaders, will not be impatient with the complexity or the incompleteness of knowledge about giftedness. We do not yet know the end of the complexity of the functioning of the human mind and personality. This book, however, is inspired by the conviction that it is high time that we begin developing the strategies, methods, and materials that have built into them an acceptance of this complexity. In large part it is derived from the author and his associates' experimental work with gifted children.

In his own studies of creative giftedness the author has continued to be increasingly impressed by the wonderful complexity of this single aspect of man's intellectual functioning. Many fascinating insights concerning the functioning of children's minds occur even when we limit ourselves to the examination of such qualities of thinking as fluency of ideas, spontaneous flexibility, originality, and elaboration. Some children are exceptionally fluent in the production of ideas expressed in words but are unable to express ideas in figural or auditory symbols. Others may be tremendously fluent in expressing ideas in figural form but appear paralyzed mentally when asked to express them in words or sounds. Similar phenomena seem to occur when we consider creative movement or kinesthetic behavior.

A child may not be able to express his ideas verbally, visually, or any other way with a great deal of fluency and yet be quite gifted in other kinds of constructive, creative behavior. He may produce a small number of ideas, but each idea may be quite original or unusual and of high quality. He may be able to take a single idea and do an outstanding job of elaborating or expanding it, or he may produce ideas which show a great deal of flexibility of thinking.

The complexity of children's creative thinking does not end here. A child might respond quite creatively to one task and barely respond to another. For example, some children show tremendous originality and elaboration on the Incomplete Figures Test and respond very poorly to the Circles Test and vice versa (Torrance, 1962a). The Incomplete Figures Text confronts the child with incomplete structures, and this produces tension in most observers, making them want to complete the structures and integrate or synthesize their relatively unrelated elements. The pages of circles of the Circles Test, however, confront the subject with "perfect structures." In order to produce pictures and objects which have as a major part a circle, the child has to disrupt or destroy these "perfect structures," the circles. In the creative process there seems to be an essential tension between the two opposing tendencies symbolized by these two tasks: the tendency toward structuring and synthesizing and the tendency toward disruption and diffusion of energy and attention. Most children seem able to express both tendencies with equal skill, but others seem able to express only one of these tendencies to any great degree.

The author has mentioned here only a few of the ways he has devised for measuring the mental abilities involved in creative thinking, yet he realizes that he has only begun to represent psychometrically the different ways children can express their creative giftedness.

Some of the Scientific Bases of Emerging Concepts

AWAY FROM CONCEPTS OF A SINGLE KIND OF GIFTEDNESS

Many educators and psychologists have been struggling for years to tear themselves away from concepts of a single type of giftedness. Undoubtedly this struggle has been motivated by vague anxieties that such concepts lead to errors and inhumane treatment for many children. The difficulty has been in finding a way to conceptualize the various kinds of intellectual giftedness and to develop measures of the different kinds of mental abilities involved. There have been numerous brave but unsuccessful attempts. For example, on the basis of the report of the Norwood Committee in England (Burt, 1958), the Education Act of 1944 in that country gave recognition to the hypothesis that there are different kinds of intellectual giftedness. Burt, in fact, maintains that the Education Act of 1944 assumes that children differ more in quality of ability than in amount. This act recommended a tripartite classification of secondary school, based on the idea that there are three main types of giftedness: a literary or abstract type to be educated at grammar schools, a mechanical or technical type to be educated at technical schools, and a concrete or practical type to be educated at modern schools. Burt argues that this scheme has not worked out as well as had been hoped. This may well be due, however, to still another oversimplification of the problem. Many believe, nevertheless, that this tripartite system in England is much more successful than earlier systems based on a single type of giftedness.

Guilford's structure of intellect (1956, 1959) and research related to the creative thinking or divergent production abilities have been especially effective in directing educators and psychologists away from their dependence upon a single measure of giftedness. Guilford has given us what amounts virtually to a periodic table of different kinds of intelligence. His theoretical model of the structure of intellect has three dimensions: operations, contents, and products.

In this model the operations are the major kinds of intellectual activities or processes, the things that the organism does with the raw materials of information. The first, *cognition*, includes discovery, awareness, recognition, comprehension, or understanding. The second, *memory*, refers to retention or storage, with some degree of availability, of information. Then there are two types of *productive thinking* in which something is produced from what has been cognized or memorized: *divergent production,* or the generation of information from given information, where emphasis is upon variety and quantity of output from the same source, and *convergent production,* or the generation of information where emphasis is upon achieving unique or conventionally accepted best outcomes (the given information fully determines the response). The fifth operation is *evaluation*, reaching decisions or making judgments concerning the correctness, suitability, adequacy, desirability, and so forth of information in terms of criteria of identity, consistency, and goal satisfaction.

These five operations act upon each of the kinds of content (figural, symbolic, semantic, and behavioral) and products (units, classes, systems, transformations, and implications).

In this book the term *productive thinking* will be used to refer to what Guilford has defined as *convergent production* and *divergent production*. The term *creative thinking* will be used to refer to such abilities as fluency (large number of ideas), flexibility (variety of different approaches or categories of ideas), originality (unusual, off-the-beaten track ideas), elaboration (well developed and detailed ideas), sensitivity to defects and problems, and redefinition (perceiving in a way different from the usual, established, or intended way or use). *Measured creative thinking ability* will be used to refer to test scores which have been devised to assess these abilities.

Guilford and his associates' monumental work remained almost totally neglected by educators until Getzels and Jackson (1962) showed that highly creative or divergent thinking adolescents achieved as well as their highly intelligent peers, in spite of the fact that their average IQ was 23 points lower. Since at least 1898, psychologists had been producing instruments for assessing the creative-thinking abilities, making pleas for using such measures to supplement intelligence tests and recommending educational changes needed to develop creative talent. In the main these earlier efforts to generate interest in creative development and other types of intellectual functioning not represented by intelligence tests were ignored or soon forgotten. Many of these earlier efforts are receiving attention now.

In selecting materials for this book, a serious effort has been made to provide ideas that can be used in teaching gifted children in both regular and segregated classrooms. The ideas presented have almost infinite possibilities for use with a variety of types of gifted children. It is to be expected that in the hands of some groups of gifted children the line of development from these methods and materials will be quite different from what will ensue in other groups. These materials and methods rarely require that specific questions be answered in a given way. It is to be hoped that teachers will not give severe disapproval when children answer questions or offer solutions to problems in a different way or ask different, more penetrating questions. Such questions and solutions are essential in many kinds of gifted performance.

Single studies such as those of Getzels and Jackson (1962) always leave many questions unanswered. Since the Getzels-Jackson data were obtained from a single school, one with an unusually large number of gifted students, their study did not tell us under what conditions their results could be anticipated. This author and his associates have undertaken fifteen partial replications of the Getzels-Jackson study, hoping to obtain some clues to answer this question. In ten of these studies the results have been essentially the same as in the Getzels-Jackson study. In the other five the high IQ group scored significantly higher than the highly creative group on tests of achievement. In general it has been our impression that the children in these five schools were taught primarily by methods of authority and had very little chance to use their creative-thinking abilities in acquiring educational skills. In most the average IQ was lower than in the schools where the Getzels-Jackson results were confirmed. These observations suggested that the phenomena Getzels and Jackson report may occur only in schools where students are taught in such a way that they have a chance to use their creative-thinking abilities in acquiring traditional educational skills or where the average IQ in the entire school is rather high.

It was observed that the highly creative pupils in at least two of the five divergent schools overachieved in the sense that their educational quotients were considerably higher than their intelligence quotients. Thus we thought that an ability gradient might be operating. According to the concept of the ability gradient suggested by J. E. Anderson (1960), ability level can be thought of in terms of thresholds, and questions can be asked about the amount of the ability necessary to accomplish a task. Then consideration can be given to the factors that determine function beyond this threshold. There are cutoff points of levels about which the demonstration of ability in relation to minimum demands is determined by other factors. In other words the creative-thinking abilities might show their differential effects only beyond certain minimal levels of intelligence.

To test this possibility, Yamamoto (1964) in one of the Minnesota studies of creative thinking, reanalyzed the data from six of the partial replications already mentioned. In each case students who scored in the top 20 per cent on the test of creative thinking were divided into three groups according to IQ (above 130, 120 to 129, and below 120). In general the achievement of the first two groups did not differ from each other but was significantly higher than that of the third group (IQ below 120). This finding supports suggestions made previously by several people, including this author (Torrance, 1962a), Roe (1960), and Mac-Kinnon (1961).

Still almost unnoticed by educators is that part of the Getzels-Jackson study (1962) dealing with two kinds of psychosocial excellence or giftedness—that is, high social adjustment and high moral courage. It was found that just as the highly intelligent student is not always highly creative, the highly adjusted student is not always highly moral. Further it was found that although the highly moral students achieved at a higher level than the highly adjusted students, the teachers perceived the highly adjusted students as the leaders rather than the highly moral ones. This is especially significant in a peer-oriented culture such as we have in the United States. It is well to recognize the dangers of giving the greater rewards to those who accept the peer-value system and adjust almost automatically to the immediate group, almost without reference to moral values.

It is the contention of the author that we can do a better job of helping children achieve excellence in both social adjustment and moral courage.

AWAY FROM CONCEPTS OF FIXED INTELLIGENCE

From time to time investigators have assaulted the concept of fixed intelligence. Despite this the view that intelligence is a capacity fixed once and for all by genetic inheritance is still held quite widely. Indeed a great deal of empirical evidence seems at first glance to support the idea of fixed intelligence. Recently, however, Hunt (1961) proposed alternative explanations and summarized evidence which undermines this hypothesis.

It has been shown that performance (scores, not IQ) on the Binet-type intelligence tests improves with age. Age-discrimination, however, was one of the criteria Binet used in selecting items. Although Binet himself (1909) regarded intelligence as "plastic," the fact that performance on tests selected on age-discrimination criteria showed improvement with age has been used to conclude that development is predetermined by genetic inheritance. Another argument has been that individual children show considerable constancy from one intelligence test to another. Since all intelligence tests traditionally have been validated against the Binet-type test, this is to be expected. It has also been shown that there are high intercorrelations among the various Binet-type tests, and this has been presented as evidence in favor of a high "g" (general ability) factor. Another argument of the adherents of fixed intelligence has been based on evidence which shows that intelligence tests are fairly good predictors of school achievement. Since curricula and achievement tests have been based on the intelligence-test concept of the human mind, this too is to be expected.

Studies involving hereditary versus environmental determination also have been used to support the idea of fixed intelligence. The evidence here, however, frequently has not supported the idea of fixed intelligence. Both hereditary and environmental influences interact in determining mental growth and educational achievement.

Hunt (1961) has summarized evidence from studies of identical twins reared apart, from repeated testing of the same children in longitudinal studies, and from studies of the effects of training or guided, planned learning experiences. He believes that studies of the constancy of the IQ within individuals pose the most serious challenge to fixed intelligence. These include studies both of the stability with which individuals maintain their positions within a given group of individuals from one testing to another testing and of the variations of IQ within specific individuals.

Studies of the effects of schooling have been fairly convincing. Out of a group of people tested at some earlier age, those who complete the most schooling show the greatest increases and fewest decreases in IQ. Hunt cites studies by Lorge (1945), Vernon (1948), and deGroot (1948, 1951). In the area of early environmental influences, Hunt mentions the sustained work of Wellman, Skeels, and their colleagues of the Iowa group. This group continued their studies over many years, demonstrating many of the effects of training at the kindergarten and nursery level. The studies of Spitz (1945, 1946) have been quite influential in convincing psychiatrists and social caseworkers that intelligence is plastic and modifiable, not fixed and that mothering is crucial during the early years of life. Children deprived of social interaction or mothering fail to develop naturally either physically or mentally.

AWAY FROM BELIEFS IN PREDETERMINED DEVELOPMENT

Long-standing beliefs in predetermined development have been used frequently to support the concept of fixed intelligence. Much evidence, however, indicates that deprivations of experience make a difference in rates of various kinds of growth. The more severe the deprivations of experience have been, the greater has been the decrease in the rates of development.

Arguments concerning inherited patterns of mental growth have also been placed in doubt by the work of Hunt (1961), Ojemann (1948), Ojemann and Pritchett (1963), and others. The evidence seems to indicate that intellectual development is quite different when children are exposed to guided, planned learning experiences from that which occurs when they encounter only what the environment just happens to provide.

This has led to the suggestion that educational programs should be based upon guided, planned experiences which in turn are based upon an analysis of the requirements of the learning task and the condition of the child. Analysis of the task must include a consideration of the structure of the task, possible strategies or processes by which the task can be achieved (alternative ways of learning, kinds of discriminations to be made, and so forth), and the settings or conditions which facilitate or impede achievement of the task (cultural, social, physical, and the like). Analysis of the child's condition should consider the stage of development relevant to the concepts or skills to be learned, the level of relevant abilities, especially the most highly developed ones (memory, logical reasoning, originality, judgments of space, and so forth), and the individual child's preferred ways of learning. The concern is with potentiality rather than norms. Examples of such educational experiences will be outlined in the section on classroom procedures.

CONCLUSION

In this chapter an effort has been made to show how recent breakthroughs in research concerning the human mind and personality and their functioning have resulted in the emergence of a new and challenging concept of giftedness. This concept stresses the importance of emphasis upon potentiality rather than upon norms and single measures of giftedness. It involves movement away from concepts of a single type of giftedness and fixed intelligence and beliefs in predetermined development. In the following chapters an effort will be made to outline educational goals, identification procedures, strategies of motivation, and methods and materials of instruction appropriate for the education of gifted children.

2

Goals in Teaching Gifted Children

NEED FOR GOALS

A GIFTED CHILD is potentially an awesomely powerful force. He can advance civilization or destroy it. The creative energies of gifted children need to be activated and guided early, or else they can be lost—or prove dangerous. Thus it is important that the classroom teacher ask "What kind of persons do I want the gifted children I teach to become?"

COMMONLY HELD GOALS

Below are five sets of characteristics which best describe five different gifted students. Which of these individuals would you want your students to become? Try ranking them from most desirable to least desirable in the blanks at the left of the descriptions.

―――― *Student 1.* Affectionate, considerate of others, courteous, does work on time, industrious, obedient, remembers well, willing to accept judgments of his elders, not bashful, does not disturb existing organization and procedures, not talkative.

―――― *Student 2.* Considerate of others, a self-starter, courteous, strong determination, independent thinker, industrious, good sense of humor, sincere, not domineering, does not disturb existing organization and procedure, not timid or bashful, curious.

―――― *Student 3.* Courageous in convictions, curious, independent in thinking and judgment, becomes absorbed and preoccupied with tasks, intuitive, persistent; unwilling to accept things on mere say-so,

willing to take risks, not willing to accept judgments of authorities.
—— *Student 4.* Socially well-adjusted, conforming to behavioral norms of his group, willing to accept judgments of authorities, obedient, courteous, prompt in doing work, neat and orderly, reserved, popular, and well liked by peers.
—— *Student 5.* Adventurous, attempts difficult tasks, curious, independent in judgment and thinking, industrious, self-confident, good sense of humor, sincere, not bashful or timid, not domineering, does not disturb existing organization and procedure.

Actually, four of the five sets of descriptions above are composites of the ideal personality suggested by different groups of teachers. The characteristics of the first student are those most valued by 147 Philippine teachers. In many ways this student is a sheer delight to have in classes taught by authoritarian methods and in many social and work groups. He is not likely to initiate projects, disagree with authorities, develop new ideas, or prove creative.

The second student is the composite ideal of over 1,000 teachers from several different states. He is likely to initiate projects and develop new ideas but is apt to experience a great deal of discomfort when such characteristics bring him into conflict with others or cause him to neglect some of the fine points of courtesy. He is the victim of a great deal of ambivalence. The third student is the composite ideal of a panel of ten students of the personalities of those who make outstanding creative contributions to our society. The fourth student embodies the characteristics rated by this panel of experts as least essential in the making of a productive, creative personality. The fifth student is the composite ideal of 93 teachers in Berlin, Germany.

These results were obtained by using the checklist of characteristics given in Appendix A. Teachers were asked to check characteristics they believe should be encouraged, double check characteristics they regard as most important and as requiring special encouragement, and strike out characteristics which should be discouraged or punished. By assigning a value of two to double checks, one to single checks, and minus one to strikeouts, an index of desirability-undesirability was obtained for each characteristic. The characteristics were then ranked. The list of characteristics was compiled by the author on the basis of over fifty which compare the personalities of outstandingly creative people with people whose personalities are similar but who have not achieved a high level of creative production.

The author and his associates have now accumulated data from several groups of teachers in the United States, including Negro teachers in segregated schools; Western Samoa; Malaya, including Chinese, Malayan, British, and Tamil teachers; India, Greece; Germany; and the Philippines. Of all of these groups, the composite ideals of the United States, German, and British teachers in that order most closely resemble that of the experts who rated the productive creative personality. This is in line with historical records of creative achievement. For example (Bloom, 1958), in the fields of physics, chemistry, physiology, and medicine the number of Nobel Prize winners (1901–1955) by country are as follows: Germany, 41; United States, 40; Great Britain, 32; France, 15; India, 1; and Japan, 1.

When the ratings of the experts of persons having outstanding creative achievements are compared with the composite ratings of the various cultural groups, it is clear that all of them have values which support creative achievement and others which are inimical to such achievement. It would appear that all of the cultures thus far studied may be unduly punishing the good guesser, the child who is courageous in his convictions, the emotionally sensitive individual, the intuitive thinker, the individual who regresses occasionally and plays or acts childlike, the visionary individual, and the person who is unwilling to accept something on mere say-so without evidence. On the other hand all of them may be giving unduly great rewards for being courteous, prompt, obedient, popular and well liked, and willing to accept the judgments of authorities.

Some Implications of the Composite Ideal of United States Teachers

It has long been the avowed aim of educators in the United States to provide the kinds of education which will permit each child to achieve his potentialities. Practically, however, both teachers and parents give evidence of being more concerned about having "good children" in the sense of their being easy to manage, well behaved, and adjusted to social norms. It is rare that we are genuinely willing for a child to achieve his potentialities. In fact, there is more concern about "appearing to be" than about "being." Achieving one's potentialities inevitably makes a child different and being different almost always brings disapproval. Even when a child is different in ways which are defined as socially desirable, he finds himself under pressure. He may study too hard and learn more than he should. He may be too honest, too courageous, too altruistic, or too affectionate as well as too adventurous, too curious, and too determined.

Let us examine briefly some of the implications suggested by each of the ten top rankings of the United States teachers.

1. *Considerate of Others.* Teachers and parents in the United States rank "being considerate of others" as the most important of the characteristics listed. The great importance attached by teachers certainly explains why they do not prefer highly creative pupils as we find in the Getzels-Jackson Study (1962). The high ranking of this characteristic by parents also suggests why creatively gifted children sometimes become estranged from their parents. Studies show that highly creative people frequently appear to be lacking in consideration of others. They may sacrifice their lives working for the good of others. There are times, however, when they become so involved in the problems which concern them that they do not have the time to appear to be polite and show their consideration for others.

Placing consideration of others at the top of our hierarchy of values may, however, reflect an overemphasis on conformity to the thinking of others and could be carried to such an extreme that it could work against the freeing of potentiality. It may also be an indication of a subtle conditioning for dishonesty, and the kind of consideration teachers and parents have in mind may be a shallow, actually dishonest kind of consideration. At any rate the high placement of consideration of others identifies an area in which creatively gifted children will need guidance. They could become less disturbing and less difficult to parents, teachers, and peers by showing greater consideration of others. Yet should they be encouraged to behave dishonestly, since any conditioning to dishonesty will inevitably diminish genuine creativity?

2. *Independent in Thinking.* Since almost all studies of creative persons stress the importance of independence in thinking, it is gratifying to note the high value assigned to this characteristic. Genuine creative accomplishment, however, requires independence not only in thinking but also in judgment. The creative person must be able to make judgments independently and stick to them, even though others do not agree. In the beginning any new idea always makes its originator a minority of one. We know only too well that being a minority of one makes a person uncomfortable. Thus independence in judgment takes great courage. Although parents value courage considerably more than do teachers, they still place courage nineteenth among the characteristics included in the checklist. In fact it is more important to parents that their children be courteous, do their work on time, be energetic and industrious, be obedient, and remember well than that they be courageous in their convictions.

3. *Determination.* Strong determination is indeed an important characteristic of the creative person. Someone has suggested that the truly creative personality is likely to be the first to give in but the last to give up. While we recognize determination as a desirable characteristic, we tend not to like

it when the determination is in opposition to our own will. Thus determination often brings creative persons into conflict with teachers, employers, parents, and other authorities. This is apparently the kind of determination necessary to the productive, creative person. Perhaps teachers and parents need to teach some determined, creatively gifted children how to *give in* occasionally *without giving up*. Less determined and creative, but otherwise gifted, youngsters need, of course, to learn greater determination in order to realize their potentialities.

4. *Industrious*.   Creative persons are never content to work a forty-hour week. They cannot stop thinking and working. In spite of the great industry and intensity with which the creative child works, parents and teachers may regard him as a daydreamer, lazy, or inconsistent. Many highly creative persons do not appear to be industrious, because they are not visibly busy. In order to free the creative thinking abilities to function, we must admit thinking to a status of legitimacy. To do otherwise is to emphasize "appearing to be" rather than genuine "being" and to condition for dishonesty. Of course, one may "appear" to be "creative" in order to justify his lack of industry.

5. *Sense of Humor*.   Creative individuals are noted for their sense of humor, but their sense of humor does not always endear them to their associates. It is likely to win for them such labels as "silly," "crazy," "clown," "cut-up," and the like. The treatment accorded creative persons frequently makes them hostile, and their hostility finds its way into their humor in the form of satire or sarcasm. One would hope that parents and teachers could appreciate the sense of humor of creative pupils and help them maintain it without becoming obnoxious through excessive silliness or hostility. Many creative children need help in reducing their hostility, while maintaining their aggressiveness, independence in judgment, and courage. Parents and teachers should recognize that creative children sometimes clown around as a defense to enable them to tolerate the discomfort which arises from being so frequently a minority of one in expressing their honest judgments and original ideas.

6. *Curiosity*.   The high place assigned to curiosity by teachers in the United States is encouraging. Curiosity is an important element in the creative personality and in the creative process. Children lacking curiosity may absorb the information they are required to learn and master the skills of reading, arithmetic, and writing but be tremendously limited in achieving their possibilities. They are not likely to be motivated to continue learning for the rest of their lives.

7. *Sincere*.   Studies show that creative personalities are extremely sincere in all that they do. Living truly and searching for the truth is almost an obsession with them. Albert Einstein was ridiculed by the nickname "Honest John." His peers thought that he was not "very bright" because he told the truth even when it got him in trouble. Parents and teachers pay lip service to the importance of sincerity and honesty, yet subtly condition children in many ways to be dishonest. Both parents and teachers should be careful to pay more than lip service when the sincere thoughts and feelings expressed by children are not all the clean and holy ones that we approve or are different from ours.

8. *Courteous*.   There are times when the creative child or adult does not appear to be courteous. He may be too honest or too busy to appear to be courteous—if not too busy with his hands, too busy with his mind. Since

courtesy is so highly valued in our society, we may have to help creatively gifted children behave more courteously so that they may survive.

9. *Doing work on time.* Promptness is highly valued in our society, and this frequently invloves the creative person in difficulties. Because creativity requires that one permit one thing to lead to another, it often entails the busy pursuit of some exciting and promising idea instead of the meeting of some deadline which is perceived as comparatively unimportant. Teachers need to recognize that there are times when a person may strain mightily for an idea and still fail despite all conscious effort. Then suddenly it just seems to "happen." The tyranny of the clock is a mighty enemy of imaginative thinking.

10. *Healthy.* United States teachers rank being healthy in tenth place and parents rank it in second place. It is easy to understand why parents rank this characteristic higher than do teachers because society has placed major responsibility for the health of children on parents and at the same time places a high value on health. In a similar manner parents place somewhat greater values than teachers on affection and courage, but neither group ranks these characteristics as high as health.

In examining the characteristics most honored by teachers in the United States, we have seen some influences which are favorable to the development of the potentialities of gifted children. It is interesting to note that only two of the characteristics most honored by United States teachers are included in the top ten characteristics in the ratings of the panel of experts of the most essential characteristics of the productive, creative person. These are curiosity and independence in thinking. Missing are intellectual courage or courageousness in convictions, independence in judgment, becoming absorbed and preoccupied with tasks, intuitiveness, persistence, unwillingness to accept things on mere say-so, willingness to take risks, and unwillingness to accept the judgments of authorities. This fact should give teachers of gifted children special cause for reassessing their values and goals in teaching such children.

INTELLECTUAL GOALS

In emphasizing in this chapter the kinds of persons gifted children may become, there is no intention to deemphasize intellectual development. In fact it is the author's contention that if we cultivate intellectual courage, independence in thinking and judgment, giving oneself completely to tasks, intuitive thinking, persistence, unwillingness to accept things on mere say-so, curiosity, and the like, we will have little worry about intellectual goals. Children will begin acquiring early the motivations and skills for learning throughout their lives. Their lives will be directed toward the development of potential rather than the achievement of behavioral norms, social adjustment, and the like.

Perhaps it would be well at this point to correct the misunderstanding of some teachers that information, memory, and the memory abilities are not important. Having a good memory and being a good thinker are quite compatible. Facts are indeed the food for thinking. Many of the great thinkers of the past were encyclopedic in their knowledge of what was known at the time in which they lived. Aristotle, da Vinci, Newton, and Darwin were noted for the vastness of their knowledge. Today our store of knowledge is much greater and is increasing at ever greater rates. This creates the necessity for giving attention to knowledge-availability systems, as well as continued efforts throughout one's lifetime.

The development of judgment, critical thinking, and decision-making skills is also important. It has been the author's experience in working with gifted children that many of them are inhibited in producing ideas by overdeveloped habits of criticism. It would, of course, be unwise to encourage children to produce unusual ideas without developing habits and skills of testing and evaluating them.

What we should be concerned about is the development of all of the gifted child's intellectual abilities. Guilford (1961) maintains that the human organism acquires information, retains it, uses it in generating new information, and evaluates information at each of these steps. Thus, while we should be concerned that gifted children acquire a great deal of information and retain it, we should not be greatly disturbed if they show little inclination to become walking encyclopedias. Teachers of gifted children should be concerned about what kind of persons their students are becoming. What kind of thinking do they engage in? How resourceful are they? Can they direct their own goals and initiate their own learning? Are they learning to give thoughtful explanations of things they see, hear, and do? Do they consider their ideas important? Do they relate similar experiences together to draw conclusions? Do they do some thinking for themselves? Teachers and parents can use these questions as a guide in helping the gifted child develop his potentialities.

3

Identifying Gifted Children

ACCEPTANCE of the complex concept of giftedness discussed in the first two chapters commits one unalterably to complexities in identifying gifted children. The procedures, means, and goals for identifying gifted children under this complex concept become clear when the task is seen as one of searching for indications of unusual potentialities which, if given intelligent guidance and encouragement, can result in outstanding achievements of value to society. In fact such an approach is actually freer of confusion than the many current procedures that seek to establish some single index of giftedness for use in an almost legalistic way in selecting children for special programs, scholarships, and the like. In this and succeeding chapters an effort will be made to show how this approach can serve as a useful and practical guide in helping gifted children achieve their potentialities.

Why Identification Is Important

ARGUMENTS AGAINST IDENTIFICATION

Many people strongly oppose the identification of giftedness in children. Some people believe that identifying a child as "gifted" is like placing a curse upon him. Others believe that the damage is not to the child who is identified as gifted but to those who are not so identified. Others argue that it is futile to identify giftedness in children, because giftedness will somehow come out of a person if he is gifted. They argue that gifted people have always met opposition, ridicule, and scorn and that they always will. Thus no matter how innately gifted they might be, this giftedness is of no social importance unless the person is able to prevail against these forces.

The author's own observations have convinced him that these arguments are false and lead to dangerous consequences. For example, in our longitudinal studies of creatively gifted children, we have seen children in the process of sacrificing needlessly what promised to be great creative talents. It is true that some of them will sacrifice their creativity only for a while and will regain it when they learn better how to cope with coercive pressures. It is apparent, however, that some never regain the creativity they showed so richly in the third grade. Instead they choose the paths of delinquency, mental illness, or at best a life of mediocrity and unrealized possibilities.

CHANGED BEHAVIOR INDUCED BY IDENTIFICATION

In our longitudinal studies we also have seen dramatic changes take place in the functioning of a child identified as being creatively gifted. During the first year of these longitudinal studies the author was told by most fourth-, fifth-, and sixth-grade teachers that they had some pupils who could not take a test of creative thinking because they could not read or write. Usually we tested these children individually and orally. In some cases they were tested both with group and individual tests. In almost every class at least one of these "hopeless cases" turned out to be creatively gifted in some way. When this was discussed with the teacher, he usually showed curiosity concerning the potential of the pupil, started asking him questions he would ordinarily never have dared ask, and giving him assignments to test his potentiality. Almost always the teacher was amazed that the pupil knew so much, thought so deeply, and could produce such excellent solutions to problems. In some cases such occurrences became turning points in a child's school career.

IDENTIFICATION AS BASIS FOR INDIVIDUALIZING INSTRUCTION

Some teachers and laymen argue that it is useless to identify giftedness because "what is good for the average is good for all." This argument is simply not true. The results of practically every educational experiment that has taken into consideration different levels and kinds of ability provide an argument in favor of the importance of individualized instruction. It is true that in most classrooms the so-called "average" may demand most of the teacher's time and effort. This leaves the problem of motivating and guiding the learning and thinking of those who are different from the average.

Whether we are concerned about identification of giftedness as a basis for individualizing instruction within a classroom, grouping children for instruction, or acceleration, an effort should be made to consider the kinds of giftedness that make a difference in the way children should be taught. One of the major reasons why the author has been interested in developing measures of the creative-thinking abilities is that he believes they provide one useful basis in differentiating instruction for different kinds of gifted children. Since abilities at least to some extent constitute a basis of needs and motivations, knowledge about a child's creative-thinking abilities seems to reveal differential preferences for ways of learning.

A variety of convergent bits of evidence from the research of investigators such as McConnell (1934), Stolurow (1962), Burkhart (1962), and Hutchinson (1961) support the conclusion that whenever the way of teaching children is changed, different children become the star learners and thinkers. Similarly, whenever methods of assessing the outcomes of educational experiences are changed, different children emerge as the stars. Stolurow, for example, found that with certain strategies of programming instruction, posttraining achievement is more closely related to measures of originality than to measures of mental age derived from intelligence tests. Hutchinson (1961), by changing regular classroom instruction to give opportunities for different kinds of mental functioning, obtained similar results.

MOTIVATIONAL EFFECTS OF IDENTIFICATION

Before dismissing the role of identification, a few observations should be made concerning the motivational effects of identification among gifted children. While there is a lack of controlled studies concerning this problem, there is a great deal of evidence indicating that identification and recognition programs can exercise powerful motivating influences on gifted children. An interesting example of such a program is the Bausch & Lomb

Honorary Science Awards and Science Scholarships. In 1959, Bausch & Lomb made available to the author a file of letters from award recipients and a copy of the company's follow-up studies. It is clear that many of these gifted young people who later achieved distinguished careers in the sciences would not have considered college education or careers in science, except for this recognition.

Spencer (1957) has reported some interesting outcomes from a statewide identification project in Oklahoma. As soon as the results of the program were available, the chairman of the Oklahoma Frontiers of Science Foundation sent a letter to the seven thousand bright children identified through the project. One result was that the following fall there was an increase of around 27 per cent in enrollment in science classes in schools that had participated in the program. There was even a 14 per cent increase in enrollment in science and mathematics courses in schools not participating the program. Influences on the individual lives of gifted children were even more touching. One gifted girl in an orphanage showed her letter to an aunt and within a month the aunt and uncle adopted her. This could have been done at any time during the previous several years, but apparently the identification letter produced this major change. The result was that another gifted child received an opportunity to realize her potentialities. Some high-school students who had stopped taking science and mathematics courses resumed them and have since gone on to distinguished careers in college.

CURRENT PRACTICES IN IDENTIFYING GIFTED CHILDREN

MOST COMMON PRACTICES

As Gallagher (1964) points out in his book on teaching the gifted child, the means of identifying gifted children during the first two decades of the century was teacher nomination. In many places this is still the sole or chief method. Where nomination is heavily relied upon, teachers often are given various kinds of checklists of characteristics to help them see outstanding potentialities which might otherwise be missed. In most places, however, teacher judgment has been virtually replaced by standard tests of mental ability, usually known as intelligence, or "IQ"

tests. One common practice is to use teacher nominations and/or scores derived from group intelligence tests as a means of screening children for more intensive psychological testing. These more intensive testing programs usually include achievement tests, personality tests, an individual intelligence test such as the Stanford-Binet or the Wechsler Intelligence Scale for Children, and interviews. In spite of the many discussions concerning the limitations of intelligence tests, however, most special programs for gifted children about which this author has been able to obtain data still use rather rigid cutoff points such as IQ's 130, 135, 150, or 160.

SOME RECOMMENDED PRACTICES

A number of local, state, and regional agencies have studied problems of identifying gifted children and have formulated recommendations for programs. One such agency is the Southern Regional Education Board through its Project for Education of the Gifted, headed by Virgil Ward (1962). This group found attention being given to the following seven types of data as indicators of giftedness:

1. group intelligence test.
2. teacher judgment.
3. school record, including achievement test scores, and teacher grades.
4. individual intelligence test administered by a qualified person.
5. appraisal of social and emotional maturity and adjustment.
6. parent interviews.
7. pupil ambition and drive.

In its manual on program improvement for the gifted student, Ward's committee recommended that selection should not be based on group intelligence tests alone. They suggested that teacher judgments may be useful but that teachers have a tendency to recognize as gifted the child who is attractive, well behaved, ambitious, and conforming and fail to see the potentialities of creative children who may be less mannerly, attractive, well behaved, and conforming. In using school records, the Ward group cautioned that poor teacher marks should not used in excluding a child from programs for gifted children the child shows signs of giftedness on the basis of intelligence tests, standardized achievement tests, and the like. They recommended that individual intelligence tests be used to on the validity of group intelligence tests. They suggested

parents can supply valuable information for use in identification, especially where young children are concerned. Without making any recommendation, the Ward group pointed out that some successful programs for gifted children have depended upon self-identification. Such programs admit any child who wishes to try, but he will be dropped or permitted to withdraw if he is unable to maintain the standards of the group.

A number of programs have continued to rely upon teacher identification and have tried to improve the accuracy of the judgments of teachers. The guidance materials supplied by one such group cautions that teachers tend to err in identifying gifted children because they overestimate the intelligence of glib, docile, attractive children, confuse conformity with giftedness, fail to take into account the child's background, and mistake a child who has been coached, pushed, and pressured by his parents for a child who is naturally creative and mentally alert. They also caution that some pupils who have potential ability may have failed to develop it for such reasons as: getting off to a poor start in the early grades due to absences, frequent changes in residence, or boring books; concealing ability to avoid being called "a brain" or "an egghead"; various kinds of cultural, physical, or social deprivation.

In the most successful programs for gifted children with which the author is familiar, those responsible for them have usually decided what kind or kinds of giftedness they want to cultivate, selected students on this basis, and set about trying to develop programs which will capitalize upon the characteristics of giftedness which have been used in selection.

SOME OTHER PROPOSALS FOR IDENTIFYING GIFTEDNESS

With our expanding concept of giftedness and with the development of more effective tests of mental abilities not now adequately sampled in intelligence tests, we soon should have available instruments that will be of more help than those currently in use. If we are concerned about identifying potentialities and developing them, however, we will always have to depend upon something more than test scores. Test data are useful primarily in helping teachers, counselors, and others see possibilities

in children that might otherwise be missed. Low performance on certain tests should not blind us to potentialities.

On the basis of emerging knowledge about mental abilities and giftedness, the author would like to outline several ideas which may be useful in developing ways of identifying gifted children.

1. For some time to come intelligence tests will continue to be useful in identifying and guiding gifted children, but such tests should be supplemented by observations of behavior and by other types of tests such as tests of creative thinking. The traditional lumping together in our thinking of talent, creativity, conformity, and social adjustment has resulted in identification devices saturated with conformity. In many situations outside of the classroom, performance on such devices may actually be negatively related to gifted performance. The requirements of the classroom are often so different from those of the outside world that "the rules of the game seem to have changed." Hoch (1962), Taylor (1964a), and others have pointed out that Terman's gifted subjects (based on IQ) were highly successful in their educational careers but few of them manifested their giftedness through creative contributions.

2. The basis for identifying giftedness should be relevant to the nature of the educational program provided for them. For example, there is much evidence to indicate that the relationship between measures of intelligence and creative ability is so low that identification of gifted children based on measures of intelligence alone misses large proportions of the creatively gifted. In fact, the author's own data indicate that about 70 per cent of them would be missed. Many special programs for gifted children, however, emphasize independent learning, creative ways of learning, and creative achievement. Creative, independent children would doubtless welcome the special opportunities available in such programs more than would the merely high IQ getter and would thrive on such opportunities. On the other hand it would be quite unfortunate to identify creatively gifted children and offer them educational opportunities which emphasized learning by authority, sticking to the curriculum, doing work on time, purposeless drill, and acceleration.

3. Types of giftedness other than creativeness are likely to be overlooked in classroom situations. Many teachers tend to give credit only for what children are able to write down, especially from the fourth grade onward but sometimes earlier. Even gifted adults differ greatly in their ability to transmit their ideas to writing. Teachers are also likely to overlook certain types of gifted children if they assume that only those children are gifted who engage easily in abstract thinking and therefore respond well to methods of instruction that rely on conceptual and theoretical procedures. This leads to an underestimation of children who are not very enthusiastic about abstract conceptual thinking and yet may be highly responsive and resourceful when given concrete tasks and problems from everyday life. Such children may be able to carry out quite complicated trains of thought, if they are allowed to work in a realistic world.

4. Quite obviously giftedness can be identified most effectively when children are placed in situations that require gifted behavior. There have always been a few children who have manifested their giftedness clearly

and unmistakably. For example, Isadora Duncan started teaching her unique form of modern dancing professionally at seven, and at ten, with her mother's permission, gave up school to give full time to her teaching (Goertzel and Goertzel, 1962). While still in elementary school, Fermi designed electric motors which worked. Vera Brittain wrote novels on scrap paper from her father's pottery factory while she was in elementary school.

Although such gifted performances by children are more common than generally assumed, they are not common enough to be of great service in identifying gifted children. A teacher might achieve some of the same advantages, however, by creating classroom situations that call for certain types of gifted performance. Taylor (1964b) has offered a number of very exciting illustrations of how teachers can create such situations to identify creatively gifted children. The following are a few examples:

a. At times let students do most of the planning on their own and make their own decisions and observe which ones are most dependent and which ones have the least need for training and experience in self-guidance.

b. Develop exercises through which children report their inner feelings and impulses and then have them see how well they can intuitively anticipate a correct course of action. (Example: Which is the quickest way to go from school to some remote part of the city, town, or county?) Then check accurately to see whose hunches were best.

c. Pose complex issues and see which children take a hopeful attitude rather than a position that things are in an impossible state of affairs and nothing can be done about them. Creative children stick with difficult and frustrating learning tasks.

d. Have idea-generating sessions to see who comes up with the most ideas, whose ideas bring out the strongest negative reactions from their classmates, and who tends to lead in expressing strong negative reactions. Observe who has the most courage to hold his ground or even move ahead, instead of retreating or giving up in the face of negative reactions.

e. Ask students to do a task they have done before, but take away most of the facilities previously available to see who will be the most resourceful in improvising or in accomplishing the task without the usual facilities.

f. Structure some classroom task where those who tolerate uncertainty and ambiguity do better than those who are unable to do so—in other words a situation in which the rewards go to those who keep the problem open and keep working on it with their own resources until they eventually attain a solution.

These are examples of the countless opportunities teachers can create and use in evoking and identifying the kinds of behavior that will reveal glimpses of potentialities. A teacher could not even identify outstanding jumping ability if he depended only upon his observations of how high children just happen to jump in ordinary activities. In order to identify children with outstanding jumping ability, he must create a situation that will motivate and require them to jump.

4

Motivating Gifted Children To Learn

ALTHOUGH the term *underachiever* seems woefully inappropriate in the light of new insights concerning the measurement of mental abilities and achievement, there is no question but that many gifted children are not motivated to learn and learn little, no matter how their achievement is assessed. Somehow there must be a will to learn.

It is not very helpful to explain the gifted child who is unmotivated to learn by saying that he is "lazy," "indifferent," "uncooperative," "spoiled," or "bad." There are many reasons why teachers should be concerned about such children, even in the early grades. Research indicates (Frankel, 1961) that once a pattern of "underachievement" has been established, it generally continues and becomes worse. The eventual outcome too frequently is delinquency, school dropout, and mental illness.

DEFINITION OF MOTIVATION

Research and theory concerning problems of motivation are so complex that it would be easy to become bogged down just trying to define motivation. Thus the author has defined motivation very simply as involving all those variables that arouse, sustain, and direct behavior—in our case, the learning of gifted children. This means that a gifted student lacking motivation is not sufficiently aroused and sustained to learn at anything near the level of which he is capable.

It is, of course, quite difficult to tell whether a particular child is learning at the level of which is capable, because it is practically impossible to determine what is the potentiality of a child if he is not motivated to perform well on the test or other indicator of potential. Yet it is important that teachers give attention to every indicator of potential available to them. Without a knowledge of potential, teachers may place too much pressure on a child who is already too strongly motivated and is unable to learn because he is overanxious, or be unconcerned about a potentially brilliant student whose achievement is only mediocre.

History is filled with accounts of eminent men and women, unquestionably gifted, who did not achieve very well during certain periods of their school careers. Albert Einstein, Franklin D. Roosevelt, John F. Kennedy, and Sir Winston Churchill are examples of men who at times appeared to be unmotivated to learn what their schools offered and made "C's." Wernher von Braun, the famous space scientist, failed his high-school courses in mathematics and physics. Of course, after he became enthusiastic about rocketry, he excelled in mathematics and physics. Thomas Edison's teacher thought that he was mentally "addled" and his mother withdrew him from school and taught him herself. Edison was motivated to continue to learn throughout his life and contributed numerous inventions even after he was eighty years old.

Actually it is sometimes difficult to distinguish the gifted child who is not motivated to perform well from average or slow-learning children. This difficulty is beautifully illustrated in some of the experiences of Ronald J. Goldman, educational psychologist at the University of Reading in England. He and his wife have been operating a youth club for adolescents of average and below average ability. The school records of these youngsters indicated that their IQ's are quite low—around 75 to 90—and that they were very low achievers. Besides this most of them had been engaging in considerable vandalism and hoodlum-type behavior. After working with them in the club for some time and exposing them to a stimulating and responsive environment, Dr. Goldman asked them to take an intelligence test and to do as well as they could with it. Apparently they were motivated then to perform in terms of their potential. The results showed that the average IQ of the group was about 25 points higher than their school records showed.

In a simple way the author will sketch what he regards as some of the most important reasons why unmotivated gifted children are so poorly motivated.

No Chance to Use What Is Learned

Perhaps the most fundamental cause of low motivation for learning is failure to give students a chance to use what they learn as tools in their thinking. Thus students are unable to see that school learning leads to something worthwhile and are thereby robbed of the most important and powerful reward of learning. This leaves them unmotivated and unexcited about learning. What the author has in mind is an inner stimulation that is sometimes referred to as "intrinsic motivation."

To many teachers motivation means the application of external pressures to promote some type of desirable behavior. This may be due to the emphasis that has been placed in educational psychology on the stimulus-response approach to teaching. It has been the author's experience that external pressure rarely promotes desirable behavior in unmotivated learners. In fact we can seldom "make" a student learn, behave, study, or apply himself, if he chooses not to do so.

Even if external pressures succeed temporarily, they do not supply the inner stimulation necessary for continued motivated learning. Such motivation is short-lived and requires continuous reapplication. If there is inner stimulation and the more intrinsic kinds of rewards are present, such repetition of rewards and punishments is unnecessary. Although rewards are erratic as motivators, the author is more concerned about the use of punishment to motivate gifted children than he is about rewards. Many observers of teacher behavior, even in special classes for gifted children, report that they are constantly amazed at the hostile and punitive behavior of teachers in the classroom.

Let me cite an actual case of an unmotivated gifted child who has apparently been victimized by punitive approaches to motivation. The story of this student is best told through excerpts from letters I received from his mother.

He is now thirteen years old and has had a steadily declining academic record which ended in his being retained in the seventh grade this year. . . . He has a burning *main* interest in electronics and rocks and believe me, his knowledge and interest in these two subjects is great.

His teachers, principals, and counselors have told me a confusing variety of things (confusing to me anyway). They all agree he is very bright, very bored (daydreams in class constantly), and very withdrawn though not rebellious: Two teachers have told me the school has destroyed his desire to learn. One teacher told me the school cannot help him because the only "special cases" they are informed enough to help are the "slow" children. Another teacher said to me: "I'll make him work if I have to break his spirit to do it—and ridiculing and shaming him is the only way with children like him. . . ." Last spring the school counselor and principal decided that flunking him was the only way to make him "buckle down and work or else. . . ." He can't join the different types of science clubs because he doesn't have a B average—to which the principal urged that he take up football.

So many doors closed! Where is the spirit of educating and cultivating the child's natural desire to learn—some seed of it is always there, to some extent or another!

Now, I will tell you of the boy I know, my son. . . . He is an irresponsible scatterbrain—he just can't harness his brain to such unimportant things as taking out the trash when he's hot on the trail of discovering perpetual motion. He *never* daydreams, *loves* to learn, and is always getting books from the library. He is a hard worker; many times he almost collapses trying to work and experiment late in the night. He has energy enough for ten people. He has an outgoing, bubbling personality and a terrific sense of humor. All this he is at home and in the rest of the world *until* he gets to school.

He speaks of wanting to go to an "electric college" but says he'll probably quit school when he's sixteen.

I feel that he is in a steel box—I think he feels he is too and thinks the only way to be free is to get out by quitting.

How can doors be opened, can you tell me? Can you advise or suggest *anything* that could help?

Please, don't be too busy to care or answer me. I just don't know where else to turn!

Problems such as the one just presented would doubtless be much rarer than they are, if we devoted more effort to motivating learning by providing more experiences in school for doing something with what has been learned. Some of the new curricular materials in mathematics, physics, chemistry, and other fields should make it easier for teachers to provide such experiences. Such experiences capitalize upon the disciplined use of curiosity, learning to draw suggestive inferences from minimum data, a habit of searching for relationships and analogies, and honest use of evidence.

INTEREST IN WHAT IS LEARNED RATHER THAN GRADES

Many gifted children are keenly aware of the shallowness and inadequacies of the grading systems to which they are subjected. They would doubtless be more strongly motivated to learn, if their teachers and parents were more interested in what they are actually learning and achieving rather than how well they do on a particular test. This predicament can, of course, be remedied somewhat by the development of more adequate ways of assessing the outcomes of learning experiences. The addition of tests that require creative problem-solving, decision-making, judgment, new organizations and syntheses of data, and the like would help.

Even discounting the inadequacies of present-day achievement tests, we find some interesting clues in the discrepancies between the teacher grades of some gifted children and their performance on difficult scholarship tests. Drews (1961b) identified three types of gifted high-school students: social leaders, studious achievers, and creative intellectuals. Of these, the studious achievers attained the highest teacher grades and the creative intellectuals, the lowest. The creative intellectuals, however, excelled the other two groups on difficult standardized achievement tests, sampling a wide range of content and educational skills. During the usual preparation period just before examinations the social leaders were studying for the first time those things on which they would be graded, though they read very little in general. The studious achievers were also studying those things that would earn them good teacher grades. The creative intellectuals, however, might be reading a book on philosophy or a college textbook, none of which would earn them credit in the teacher's grade book.

Many conversations with parents and teachers of gifted children reveal a startling confusion about actual learning or achievement and the conformity behavior necessary for attaining a passing grade. For example, one third-grade teacher complained that a certain gifted girl was failing. She remarked that she could not understand why the child was failing because she was very bright, very active, and very alert. She further commented that in an arithmetic bee she outdid the best arithmetic students in the class. She was reading books well above her grade level. She could hold the class spellbound with her stories and could set any of her classmates down in a spelling bee. This teacher, with her emphasis on conformity to behavioral norms, could not recognize that this child had perhaps learned more than any of her other pupils.

LEARNING TASKS TOO EASY OR TOO DIFFICULT

If learning tasks are consistently too difficult or too easy, gifted students will be unmotivated and as a result will learn little. Let us examine first the case of a gifted boy whose teachers consistently tried to keep his learning tasks too easy. It was not until Ted entered senior high school that it was discovered that somehow his IQ and his classroom number had been interchanged on his cumulative record during his elementary-school years. Ted's mother and older brother were aware that Ted was being treated as a mentally retarded child during his junior high-school years. He was always being downgraded or ignored by teachers. He was discouraged from undertaking difficult projects. His junior high-school science teacher told Ted's older brother that Ted had no ability for science and should be discouraged in his science interests. A nearby college-physics teacher gave Ted some guidance, however, and this teacher remarked on several occasions that he wished that his science majors knew as much science as Ted knew at the time he was in the seventh and eighth grades. It was also at this time that Ted won first place in his region and in the state science fair for his linear accelerator with which he did biological research.

Ted's story reveals a couple of additional points on the motivation of students who are frequently classified incorrectly as slow learners. Ted received a rather low grade on his first physics examination. He could hardly believe his eyes, however, as he felt that he knew thoroughly the subject matter covered by the examination. Somehow he summoned enough boldness to talk with the teacher about his examination, explaining that his answers were compatible with certain recent experiments reported in college texts and physics journals. The physics teacher, fortunately an honest man, admitted that he did not know about these recent findings but that he would check up on them and give his answer the next day. This was a fortunate experience for Ted, but the situation in chemistry was different. The chemistry teacher insisted that they stick to the "simple, fundamental things" and would not consider some of the more recent knowledge in chemistry, even though what was being taught is erroneous.

During his junior and senior years in high school Ted won eight major national and state awards for creative achievements in science and did very well on the College Board Examinations, scoring high in science and mathematics and above average in English. Yet he was still regarded as a slow learner by everyone in school except his physics teacher. At the time one of the major awards was announced a newspaper reporter asked to interview Ted and his science teachers. The physics teacher was delighted and warmly congratulated Ted. The chemistry teacher's only remark was "This is nice but think of how many good students knew nothing of the competition."

No Chance to Use Best Abilities

Alert teachers have long been aware of the fact that when they change their methods of teaching, certain children who had appeared to be slow learners become star learners and some of the former star learners become slow learners. They have also observed that when they change the nature of the test used in assessing achievement, such as from a multiple-choice test to one requiring creative applications and decision-making, the star learners and slow learners may change positions in class rankings. With some of the recent developments relative to mental abilities, some of these formerly puzzling phenomena are becoming clarified. Many convergent lines of research make it clear that when we change methods of instruction or the nature of instructional materials, children with different kinds of mental abilities become the star learners and nonlearners. Differences in methods of evaluation or in instructional materials bring out still further differences in achievement.

Hutchinson's study (1961) helps us understand this problem.

In Hutchinson's experimental condition the methods of instruction were more nearly geared to the full range of mental abilities (divergent, evaluative, and so forth) found in the normal classroom and not the high IQ students. Classroom observations showed that there was a significantly higher proportion of productive thinking in the experimental classrooms than in the control classrooms. In the control group there was a significant correlation between mental age and the difference achieved on the subject matter test from the pretest to the posttest. In contrast there was no correlation between mental age and differences achieved on subject matter for the experimental groups. The normal classroom instruction thus seems to have been geared to bring into play the abilities measured by the intelligence test to a greater extent than in the experimental conditions. Gains for the high IQ students were not as great in the experimental groups as in the control groups.

In the experimental groups where the methods were more nearly geared to the full range of abilities and not to the high IQ students, new productive and creative stars emerged and the correlations between achievement and the measures of creative thinking rose. In one of the experimental groups three of the eight students in the lowest quartile on mental age were the creative and productive stars. Similar findings have been reported by several other investigators.

No Chance to Learn in Preferred Ways

Not only are there differences in "best abilities," but there are also differences in perferred ways of learning. Since the author is frequently misunderstood on this point, a further attempt will be made to clarify the issue. In stressing the need for permitting children to learn in creative ways, the author has not intended to imply that methods involving teaching by authority should be abolished. He maintains, however, that the weight of existing evidence indicates that man fundamentally prefers to learn in creative ways—by exploring, questioning, experimenting, manipulating, testing and modifying ideas, and otherwise searching for the truth. This does not mean that it is always good for man to learn creatively. Although the needs and abilities underlying learning in creative ways are universal enough to make this way of learning valuable for all children, creative learning should not be regarded as the exclusive method of education nor even the exclusive method of education for any one child.

It is also man's nature that he have anchors in reality, that he have structure in his environment, and that he have authorities upon whom he can depend. Just as individuals differ in the extent to which they prefer to learn creatively, they also differ in the extent to which they require authorities.

LEARNING LACKING IN PURPOSEFULNESS

Motivation may be low in some gifted children because they are asked to learn things that have little or no purpose for them. Perhaps this is one reason why so many theme-a-week experiments have turned out so poorly. Some students are not motivated to learn for high grades or to avoid failing grades. They need more of a purpose to motivate them to write than "writing to be corrected." There is much more purpose if they are writing to communicate something that they have discovered for themselves. This may be one of the reasons why students who spend most of their time reading and discussing perform as well in theme writing as students who have been subjected to a year of the theme-a-week treatment (Heys, 1962). When he discovers something new, a person seems to be motivated to tell somebody about it. This fact should be useful to teachers in motivating slow learners.

The motivating power of a purpose is illustrated in the case of Tim reported by Dinkmeyer and Dreikurs (1963, p. 65):

> Tim does well in creative work but is apt to be in such a hurry that his writing is messy. For an American history assignment, he wrote a poem about Captain John Smith which was so good that each of the other fifth grade classes wanted a copy. Thrilled by this recognition, Tim made three very neat copies for them.

As Dinkmeyer and Dreikurs comment, writing correctly and neatly took on new significance in that there was real purpose for the readability of his poem. The teacher focused on his asset, his creative work, and seized the opportunity to let him recognize for himself the value of neat work.

McKeachie (1958) identifies two methods open to the teacher in developing motivation for learning, and both are related to purposefulness. One of these involves making learning instrumental for the motives a person already has. Using this approach, we try to show students how our courses will contribute to their goals in life. The second approach involves the development of new motives for learning. The first step is to make learning satisfying, and this always involves beginning with the motives students already have. Thus we have to help unmotivated gifted students see that their learning is really useful to them. By our own enthusiasm for our subject matter we can also make our students aware of the possibilities of joy in learning. McKeachie also suggests that a variety of teaching methods is another way of motivating learning.

Conclusion

Although the motivation of gifted children is inescapably a complex problem, there are some very obvious things teachers can do to improve the motivation of gifted children. They can provide more opportunities for doing something with what is learned, be more concerned about what they are learning, adapt the difficulty of the task to the ability and experience level of the learner, teach in ways that give opportunities for using a variety of mental abilities in acquiring information, recognize and reward a variety of kinds of excellence, including social adjustment and character, and give greater purposefulness to what students are expected to learn.

While these things can be done within the framework of a stimulus-response psychology, the author believes that they will be more successful in motivating gifted children—arousing, sustaining, and directing their behavior—if carried out within the framework of a responsive environment. This calls for the most alert and sensitive kind of direction and guidance (Ferebee, 1950). It means building an atmosphere of receptive listening relieving the fears of the timid and the overtaught or overstimulated, fending off negative criticism and making the learner aware of what is good, stirring the sluggish and deepening the shallow, making sure that every sincere effort to learn brings enough satisfaction to keep the learner willing to try again, and keeping alive the zest and excitement of learning.

5

Curriculum Provisions for
Gifted Children

TRADITIONAL PROVISIONS

DISCUSSIONS concerning curriculum provisions for the gifted have for the most part been limited to three possibilities: special classes, acceleration, and enrichment (K. E. Anderson, 1960; Fleigler, 1961; Gallagher, 1960; Torrance, 1960). In the author's opinion the theory, research and experience focused on these alternatives have not given and are never likely to yield the kind of guidance needed in educating gifted children. This is especially true, if we accept the expanding and emerging concept of giftedness described in the first chapter and the goals discussed in the second chapter. In fact as we look upon efforts centered around these three alternatives in the perspective of emerging knowledge, the inadequacy and crudeness of such efforts are painfully apparent. Yet the results of these experiences and the research related to them provide us with valuable data for responding constructively to the changing conditions of today.

ABILITY GROUPING

The work with special classes and ability groupings has assumed greater homogeneity than has been warranted. If children are grouped according to any single criterion such as reading ability or mental age (intelligence), the children selected as gifted will still differ in such abilities as mathematical ability, creative thinking abilities, writing ability, and many others. As already mentioned, the author's own research indicates that among children selected for gifted programs on the basis of mental age or achievement, there is no correlation between measures of creative thinking, such as those described in the first chapter, and measures of intelligence and achievement. This research has also shown that if measures of intelligence alone are used in identifying children for special classes, 70 per cent of the most superior on measures of creative thinking will be missed. In other words, if we select for a special class the fifth-grade pupils in a school who rank in the upper 20 per cent of their class on the Stanford-Binet, Kuhlmann-Anderson, Otis, or California Test of Mental Maturity, we would not include 70 per cent of those who ranked highest on a test of creative or divergent thinking. Similarly, if selections were made on the basis of performance on the test of creative thinking, we would miss 70 per cent of those who ranked highest on the test of intelligence.

Recent years have seen the emergence of some more complex plans like the Dual-Progress Plan which is being studied at New York University (Heathers, 1960). The Dual-Progress Plan provides for individualizing instruction for the gifted, the average, and the slow. An effort also has been made to group children according to ability and achievement in some areas such as science, mathematics, and the arts—using different criteria for grouping in each area, of course. In other areas such as language arts and social studies heterogeneous groupings are used. The plan is administratively complex but certainly has some advantages theoretically. Five years have been allowed for putting the plan into action and evaluating it. Its goals are being evaluated rather broadly and the final report should be much more adequate than has been the evaluation of most curricular provisions for gifted children in the past.

In summary it must be admitted that research on ability grouping, as crude and as undifferentiated as it has been, has generally shown that the academic achievement of gifted students in narrower range ability groupings tends to be somewhat greater than in broader range ability groups (heterogeneous groups). Rather definitive surveys of grouping practices have been provided by Passow (1958), Shane (1960), and K. E. Anderson (1960). Results have not been uniformly favorable, however, and many important goals of educating gifted children have

not been considered in these evaluations. The results certainly indicate that ability grouping does not solve automatically the problems of individualizing instruction.

ACCELERATION

Provisions for acceleration have never been very widespread
and have been rather generally opposed by both professional educators and laymen. The research results concerning the effects of
acceleration are rather generally favorable, as has been revealed
by a number of rather definitive surveys (K. E. Anderson, 1960;
Reynolds, 1960; Gowan, 1958). Terman (1954) and Pressey
(1954) have long advocated acceleration. Acceleration has taken
the form of early entrance to kindergarten or first grade, grade-
and junior high-school acceleration, and advanced placement or
acceleration into college. Successful projects at each of these
levels have been reported. Although the evaluation of the outcomes of these projects has taken into consideration such factors
as social adjustment as well as academic achievement, none of
these programs has been evaluated in terms of broader concepts
of intellectual functioning and the other goals discussed in the
second chapter. In fact the primary goal of acceleration usually
has been to move students along the educational ladder more rapidly or to get them out of an unchallenging and personally
damaging situation.

ENRICHMENT

Most generally approved among the three curriculum alternatives has been enrichment. Its advocates, however, have not been
able to produce as good research support as have the advocates
of special groups and acceleration (Torrance, 1960). In practice
the concepts of the enrichment ideal generally have not been
well implemented. Many who reject special grouping and acceleration believe that something more than acceleration is
needed. Perhaps one of the needs is to differentiate what is enrichment for what type of child and what is enrichment for less
able children. Perhaps another need is to provide plenty of opportunities with unlimited possibilities and to challenge the potentialities of different kinds of gifted children.

It is the author's hypothesis that sound educational opportunities for gifted children can be provided under all three of the

alternatives discussed above. The ideas suggested and described in this chapter and the remainder of this book can be adapted for use under either alternative.

SOME PROMISING CURRICULUM FRONTIERS FOR GIFTED CHILDREN

It seems to the author that educational practices traditionally have held back gifted children, especially in those areas in which they really excelled, and have tried to coerce them into becoming more versatile and well-rounded by emphasizing the development of their poorest abilities or more severe disabilities. In a speech before the Association of Educators of Gifted Children the author (1961) described the situation as an effort to "make flying monkeys abandon such antics" and to "make silent lions roar." At the time the author suggested that we change tactics, encouraging the "monkey to fly" and permitting the "silent lion to keep silent," capitalizing upon abilities more important than roaring ability. These suggestions will be summarized in this chapter.

SELF-INITIATED LEARNING

One of the most promising curriculum frontiers for educating gifted children is self-initiated learning. Provisions for self-initiated learning are necessary in implementing the concept of the responsive environment and giving children experiences in responding constructively instead of just adapting to whatever happens.

Making provisions for self-initiated learning among gifted children does not mean that they work without guidance and direction. Some of the children in the author's longitudinal studies of creative development are masters at self-learning, usually outside of the curriculum, and they make excellent use of experts of many kinds. One third-grade girl wanted to learn how to knit. Her mother did not know how to knit, so she began going from door to door until she found someone who could knit and was willing to teach her. She mastered the skill quickly and easily. One fourth-grade boy, who as a second grader gave the author the clearest and most accurate explanation he has ever heard and seen of the principle of the magnifying glass, became interested in high-speed computers. He went to the experts and is now something of an expert himself on computers.

Teachers hesitate to encourage gifted children to pursue self-initiated learning activities because this makes the curriculum different for each child who initiates a project of his own, because such achievements are difficult to evaluate, or because they do not feel competent to give the guidance needed. Self-initiated learning activities can be used successfully in both special grouping and enrichment plans. Such activities are a vital part of the Strengths and Weaknesses Program of the High Achievers Project already described. They are also a vital part of the teaching repertoire of some of the most effective elementary and secondary teachers known by the author.

If the acquisition of the motivations and skills to continue learning throughout one's life is regarded as a part of the curriculum, then concern about making the subject matter the same for all children in a class is reduced. Fears about differences in content can also be reduced, if teachers will give gifted children a chance to communicate their self-initiated learning to the entire class. This is important because a person has a strong desire to communicate to others what he finds out through self-initiated activities and it thereby becomes more meaningful. This requires, of course, that the teacher occasionally permit gifted students for a time to become the teachers of the class. It gives the teacher an opportunity to show how excited he can be about learning and that he regards as important the things that his pupils learn through their self-initiated activities. It also becomes the role of the teacher to help the student gain access to the experts needed as "alter teachers." Most teachers would be surprised to discover how willing even the ablest experts are to embrace the opportunity to teach gifted children who want to learn something that they know.

LEARNING ON ONE'S OWN

Another curriculum frontier for gifted children is the provision for gifted children to do things on their own and to learn on their own tasks assigned by the teacher. The author (1964) has shown that it is possible to encourage children to do a great deal of writing on their own by mimeographing a magazine containing their best work. In another study (Fritz, 1958) it was found that gifted seventh-grade children in heterogeneous classes in a split-shift school showed more growth in language development, science, and social studies than did equally gifted children under a full-day school. Only in spelling was there significantly less growth among the split-shift students. In still another (Torrance, 1964) it was found that children in a split-shift school engaged in a larger number of creative activities on their own than children under full schedules.

There are times when the teacher would be wise to leave most of the planning of an activity to students. Let them plan in advance and make their own decisions.

ACADEMIC DISCIPLINES AS WAYS OF THINKING

In recent years a number of the professional associations have developed curriculum materials which place emphasis upon their fields of specialization as ways of thinking rather than as accumulated bodies of knowledge. These innovations are not limited to gifted children, but represent an exciting development for them and are giving rise to new kinds of gifted children. New curriculum materials have already been developed by the Physical Science Study Committee (PSSC), the School Mathematics Study Group (SMSG), the American Chemical Society's curriculum projects, the University of Illinois Mathematics Project, and the American Institute of Biological Sciences Curriculum Study Group. New materials are being developed in the social sciences, the humanities, languages, and art. Learning by discovery and direct observation is a key to the teaching approach being developed in these materials. Children are being taught to become sensitive to problems and to the gaps in their knowledge and to inquire into ways that will yield solutions to problems and fill gaps in their knowledge. They learn to keep records of their observations and use information in solving other problems. They work with raw data and generate and test ideas from these data.

Through these curriculum revisions children are being exposed to mathematics as mathematicians see it, physics as physicists see it, and history as historians see it. A summary of most of the current curricular innovations will be found in Rosenbloom's *Modern Viewpoints in the Curriculum* (1964).

As schools have experimented with these new curriculum materials, it has become apparent that some students who were mediocre achievers become the high achievers and vice versa. When statistical studies were made to evaluate some of the outcomes of the PSSC physics, it was noted that the usual predictors of achievement could no longer be used with much success. Ornstein (1961) has reported some of the results obtained by the Educational Testing Service in their 1958–59 study of the new physics materials. He reports that a substantial number of students who had scored only slightly better than average on the School and College Aptitude Test made gradually higher scores on the special physics tests given during the year. Many of these students scored higher than a large number who were at the top on the predictor tests and presumably were specially gifted. One possible explanation is that the students whose high aptitude scores did not correlate with their achievement test scores prefer to learn by authority and are better at remembering facts and formulas than in the intuitive thinking required by the new approach. Different abilities are involved when instructional materials call for creative ways of learning.

THE RESPONSIVE ENVIRONMENT

Another important curriculum frontier which may be of special service to gifted children is being opened up through experiments in creating responsive environments through which children are propelled by their curiosity. This concept of the responsive environment is illustrated in the experimental work of Moore (1961). Through the natural curiosity of children about electric typewriters, Moore has demonstrated that preschool children can learn to read, type, and take dictation without being pushed or forced. Here we have skills being learned in creative ways—skills we have assumed can be taught most economically by authority.

REVISED CONCEPTS OF READINESS

Educators of gifted children, once they cease their "holding back operations," have to revise many of their concepts of "readiness" and what can be taught at various ages or educational levels. This frontier has already caused much concern, as indicated by the following newspaper headlines which appeared in the early 1960's:

Caution Urged in Changing Primary into High Schools
Don't Turn Grade Schools into High Schools, Educators Warn at Parley
Reading for Kindergarten, Languages Too Soon Attacked.

About readiness, Bruner (1960) writes:

Experience over the past decade points to the fact that our schools may be wasting precious years by postponing the teaching of many subjects on the grounds that they are too difficult . . . The essential point often overlooked in the planning of curricula . . . (is that) the basic ideas that lie in the heart of all science and mathematics and the basic schemes that give form to life and literature are powerful.

For this purpose Bruner suggests "the spiral curriculum," one that turns back on itself at higher and higher levels of complexity. With gifted children, some aspects of the curriculum can be grasped at higher levels of complexity than has hitherto been thought possible.

It is characteristic of highly creative people that they attempt tasks that are too difficult for them. They have developed the ability to cope with failure and frustration which inevitably results from this tendency. Had they not attempted such tasks, it is quite unlikely that their great ideas would have been born. The teacher of gifted children should at least occasionally confront them with problems that are too difficult to solve and help them develop the skills for coping with such problems. Without such opportunities, children cannot test the limits of their abilities.

SEARCH FOR SELF AND ONE'S UNIQUENESS

Generally people believe that the elementary period is too early for children to start developing their self-concepts, to start searching for their selves. The trouble is that the process is well under way even before the child enters school. Gifted children are quite concerned by this problem and are likely to be confronted with much contradictory information about themselves. A failure to help them develop clear and realistic self-concepts blocks access to important and exciting frontiers. Gifted children need help in accepting themselves because they may even despise an outstanding "gift," if this giftedness makes them different from their peers. This makes far too many gifted children willing to emasculate themselves and consciously and unconsciously hide or destroy their talents.

OPENING UP THE FRONTIERS

The following chapters will describe some specific ideas for opening up the promising frontiers in curriculum provisions for gifted children. A few general ideas which should pervade all work with gifted children will be sketched quite briefly in the remainder of this chapter.

REWARDING VARIED TALENTS

Educational research has shown repeatedly that people will develop along whatever lines they find rewarding. Thus the need for rewarding a diversity of talents, ways of learning, educational achievements, and the like is obvious.

HELP CHILDREN RECOGNIZE THE VALUE OF THEIR TALENTS

Teachers will be unable to open up curriculum frontiers for gifted children until they can help them value their potentialities and realize what some of their potentialities are. Otherwise even gifted children will continue to despise their most valuable assets.

DEVELOP CREATIVE ACCEPTANCE OF LIMITATIONS

Inevitably there are limitations, within both the environment and the individual. Both must be accepted, not cynically, but creatively. In an early study of the psychology of inventors, Rossman (1931) found that this characteristic differentiates inventors from noninventors. Noninventors see only the defects in their environment. Inventors, however, take a more constructive approach, saying: "This is the way to do it."

STOP EQUATING DIVERGENCY WITH MENTAL ILLNESS AND DELINQUENCY

One of the big barriers to opening up curriculum frontiers is our practice of equating any kind of divergent behavior with mental illness and/or delinquency. In the author's studies of highly creative children there are many evidences that their parents and teachers do not understand them.

CHANGE EMPHASIS ON SEX ROLES

Overemphasis or misplaced emphasis on sex roles is a serious block to the healthy development of many talents, especially creative ones. It has been pointed out frequently that rarely do women become scientific discoverers, inventors, or composers. Overemphasis or misplaced emphasis on sex roles, however, exacts heavy tolls on the potentialities of both sexes and creates serious problems of adjustment to highly creative individuals of both sexes. Many areas of experiencing are placed off limits to children and young people because of their sex, thus reducing their awareness and their capacity to respond constructively to changes.

Creativity, by its very nature, requires both sensitivity and independence. In our culture sensitivity is definitely a feminine virtue while independence is a masculine one. Thus the highly creative boy is likely to appear to be more effeminate than his peers and the highly creative girl to appear more masculine than hers. Roe (1963), Barron (1957), and Torrance (1963a) have all cited evidence to support this conclusion.

HELP THE DIVERGENT CHILD BECOME LESS DIFFICULT

In the author's studies of creatively gifted children it is evident that many of them bring upon themselves many of their own woes. To open to them the curriculum frontiers suggested herein, teachers may have to help them become less obnoxious or difficult without sacrificing their creativity.

Teachers should help gifted children to realize that they are likely to be given more power to realize their potentialities by being considerate of others than if they neglect such behavior. They should be helped to recognize also that outstanding talents may cause others to feel threatened and make them uncomfortable and afraid. In conserving talent, the problem seems to resolve characteristics that are essential to his creativity and at the same time helping him acquire skills for avoiding or reducing to a tolerable level the pressures against him.

DEVELOP PRIDE IN THE ACHIEVEMENT OF GIFTED PUPILS

Teachers miss good opportunities for developing pride in the achievement of gifted students. We have done this in a few areas but not in those having to do with intellectual excellence. Schools have great pride in athletic teams, bands, and the like. Much is now being done to develop pride in a school's scientific talent, especially at the high-school level. Some school systems have organized elementary-school art shows. Much more could be done, however, to give recognition to schools for their development of intellectual creative talents.

REDUCE THE ISOLATION OF THE GIFTED CHILD

Much attention has already been given the problems involved in reducing the isolation of the gifted child. Isolation has been a favorite technique for coping with individuals having almost any kind of divergent characteristic. Several currents of research (Drews, 1961b; Torrance and Arsan, 1963; Durrell, 1961) suggest that various kinds of groupings, both within classes and into classes, may open up exciting curriculum frontiers for gifted children, especially those who are "different."

PROVIDE SPONSORS OR PATRONS FOR GIFTED PUPILS

Most people who have achieved creative eminence have always had some other individual who plays the role of "sponsor" or "patron." This patron or sponsor is someone who is not a member of the peer group, but possesses prestige or power in the same social system. He does several things for the gifted child. Regardless of his own views, the sponsor encourages and supports the talented individual in expressing and testing his ideas, in thinking through things for himself. He protects the individual from the counterreactions of his peers long enough to permit him to try out some of his ideas. He can keep opportunities open so that originality can occur.

EXPLOIT THE OPPORTUNITIES OF THE MOMENT

The effective teacher always looks for the high teachable moments which are quite like some of the "great moments of scientific discovery." Much discussion has ensued concerning the role of chance in scientific discovery. Certainly many great discoveries have resulted because someone exploited a chance occurrence, an unexpected incident, or the like. As teachers learn to exploit such moments and train their pupils to do so, there is no question but that unpredicted curriculum frontiers for gifted students will emerge.

DEVELOP A SPIRIT OF MISSION

Studies of outstanding men and women in various fields almost always reveal that such people seem to be impelled by some strong feeling of mission or purpose. They believe that what they are doing is tremendously important and are thereby aroused to "all-out" efforts. When learning and thinking is made to be tremendously important and worthwhile, schools will become exciting places and curriculum frontiers will unfold. Even gifted children will achieve more than we thought possible. Unsuspected potentialities will manifest themselves.

6

Setting the Stage in Kindergarten

. . . Children of five have already incorporated into their everyday thinking ideas that most of their elders will never fully assimi-
late.—Margaret Mead, *The School in American Culture* (1955)

OUR growing knowledge of intellectual and personality development points up the importance of setting the stage for
gifted behavior during the early school years, especially the kindergarten year. Special kindergartens for culturally or educationally deprived children have been envisioned as a way of
salvaging the potentialities of gifted children in this category.
There are some indications (Hunt, 1961) that children who are
seriously deprived culturally and educationally at an early age
never catch up and achieve their potentialities, even though they
are provided enriched opportunities later on. Some who are studying problems of "underachievement" maintain that many children
are serious "underachievers" at the time they enter school.

On the other hand there are gifted children who are high
achievers at the time they enter kindergarten, but whose excitement about learning is so dulled by the experience that they are
underachievers by the time they enter first grade. Some of them
reportedly regress and are unable at the end of a traumatic year
of kindergarten to do many of the things they could do at the
time they entered. In succeeding years they seem to become
slower and slower and are eventually classified as "slow learners" or "retardates."

Both of the above images doubtless have some validity and
should be of concern when we consider the education of gifted

children. Certainly the kindergarten year is tremendously important in the development of gifted children and can contribute enormously to the salvaging of exceptional talent among culturally or educationally deprived children. It is perhaps just as certain that many existing kindergarten programs would damage rather than help gifted children from culturally deprived homes. A recent study of about one hundred preschool teachers in one state using the ideal pupil checklist discussed earlier showed that their values are the least friendly to creative development of any group of educators or parents thus far studied in the United States.

It is the author's opinion that the kindergarten education of gifted children has suffered because of misunderstandings concerning the nature and potentialities of young children. Much of the knowledge about children's thinking developed by such workers as Binet (1909), Piaget (1951, 1955), and Montessori (Standing, 1962) is not widely known or accepted by teachers. Thus there are many who still believe that kindergarten-age children are not capable of thinking. Even those who acknowledge that preprimary children can think still regard them as "birdbrained," hopping from one thing to another and unable to think of any one thing for more than ten or fifteen minutes at a time.

Teachers treat children differently, depending upon their beliefs about what children are capable of doing and what characteristics should be encouraged or punished. If kindergarten children are treated as though they are "birdbrained," this is the way they will behave. If they are respected and treated as though they are capable of absorption in a task constructively, they usually will work with great absorption in solving problems for long periods of time.

Unrecognized Giftedness

Misinterpretations of giftedness and failures to recognize giftedness may produce serious behavior problems which will become increasingly difficult to overcome. This is especially true when the manifestations of giftedness involve socially disapproved kinds of behavior, such as lying, aggressiveness, and various types of nonconformity. One case in the author's files concerns a boy who was recognized by parents, pediatricians, and others as gifted before he entered kindergarten, but his giftedness was apparently misunderstood by the kindergarten teacher. The mother recalls that his *corrected* kindergarten papers were frequently marked with failing grades because he added cowboy boots or hats to the teacher's dittoed drawings or changed them more radically. Thus his imaginativeness and nonconformity were interpreted as signs of mental retardation. After being treated virtually as a mentally retarded child for a few years, he doubtless accepts this definition and behaves accordingly. Examinations by pediatricians and outside agencies continued to show that the boy was of above average or superior intelligence, and his parents were assured that he would begin learning when he found "the right teacher." After these traumatic years it would be extremely difficult for even a good teacher to repair the damage and enable this boy to achieve his potentialities.

It must be admitted that the kindergarten teacher may at times find some types of giftedness irritating and be tempted to misinterpret them and turn them into liabilities. In the remainder of the chapter an attempt will be made to describe some ideas which may be useful in avoiding this temptation.

INTEREST SPAN

When the author began including preprimary children in his studies of creative thinking, advisers cautioned to use tasks that would require no longer than ten minutes or fifteen at the very most. He respected expert opinion but was not altogether willing to accept this advice, because in his earlier work with four- and five-year-olds in religious education he had found that they could become tremendously absorbed in certain tasks for thirty minutes or longer. Thus he went ahead with an experiment which extended from kindergarten through sixth grade and which kept each class busy for about sixty minutes. Of course there was considerable variety in the activities involved.

These and similar experiences make one wonder if the theory that the child's span of attention is extremely brief does not cause parents and teachers deliberately to inculcate the "birdbrained" mentality, rushing children into some new activity every few minutes, never giving them time to think or for one idea to lead to another.

Desire for Order and Organization

Kindergarten children, especially gifted ones, are grossly underrated regarding the ability to organize their behavior. This was one of the surprising discoveries of Maria Montessori. She recognized that children wanted things to be organized but at first thought that the adult must organize them. She soon discovered that children of kindergarten age had a real interest and talent for organizing things themselves. The following reports of kindergarten teachers also indicate that, given an opportunity, children of this age are capable of organizing their time and controlling their behavior.

One kindergarten teacher related that she once had to get 28 kindergarteners to plant bulbs in containers and to clean up, all within a 30-minute period. Some of the children rushed to get their containers but several quickly said: "We won't get it done that way." Spontaneously some of the children recognized that they must act in a more organized manner in order to accomplish the task. One child suggested that they do the planting by rows, each taking a turn without rushing or pushing. After the class organized the groups to come to the back of the room, the planting was accomplished in an orderly fashion without accidents, spilled soil, or spoiled bulbs. Each one learned which side of the bulb had to be up, planted a bulb, watered the planted bulb, and set it in a dark place. All were finished before the allotted time had expired. One child remarked: "It sure pays to think."

Creative Ways of Learning

Kindergarteners are experts in the techniques of learning in creative ways because they have had more experience in learning in these ways than in learning by authority. They have not yet abandoned creative ways of learning by questioning, inquiring, searching, manipulating, experimenting, and playing—always trying to find out in their own way the truth. If they sense that something is wrong or missing, that there is something that they do not understand, they are uncomfortable until they can do something about it. So they start asking questions, making guesses, testing, revising, and retesting. When they discover something, come upon some new (to them) truth, they want to tell somebody about it. It is such a natural process. At times it is lightning quick, automatic and spontaneous. At other times we must wait patiently—and then it may come lightning quick.

Looking at Things in a Different Way

For some time the author has been familiar with deliberate methods for increasing creativity by looking at something in a different way. Synectics (Gordon, 1961), for example, stresses the principle of making the unfamiliar, familiar or the familiar, unfamiliar. One idea was sparked when a member of the team tried to imagine himself as a drop of paint, struggling to get some kind of hold on a wall which had been painted and had not been scraped or cleaned. Children use the techniques of synectics and brainstorming spontaneously and naturally all of the time.

Four- and five-year-old children can make excellent use of opportunities for investigating things afresh and anew and more thoroughly. The author learned this through experiences in reading books to this age group. Frequently, when he would read a book to a group of four- and five-year-olds they would ask immediately that he read it again. At first he thought that he had to go through the book rapidly each time, lest they become inattentive and bored. He soon discovered, however, that they wanted just the opposite. The urgent tension to get through had been satisfied, and they were prepared to examine it afresh and more thoroughly. They were not bored and did not want to be hurried. They could now savor the experience to the fullest, elaborate upon it, and think more deeply about it.

Postponement of Learning by Authority

There are times when the kindergarten teacher might as well accept the fact that children prefer to learn creatively and postpone learning by authority. An example of such a time is the day kindergarten children are first given rhythm band instruments. Most teachers are nearly driven to distraction on this day. They want to tell the children about their instruments, but they usually fail to gain attention for more than a moment. The alert and experienced teacher, however, realizes that on this day the children must be permitted to encounter their instruments creatively.

They want to feel them, smell them, look at them, tap them, and sense them in every way possible. They must discover what the instruments will do to them. After this they are ready to learn by authority. They will listen and watch.

TOLERANCE OF PERIODS OF SILENCE AND HESITATION

Work with kindergarteners has taught the author to be tolerant of moments of silence and hesitation. In administering tests of creative thinking, it was apparent that it does not pay to hurry, urge, or push children to give responses when they are hesitant. Many of the hesitant children become quite responsive when told that "it is just for fun." When they find that the examiner takes down whatever they tell him, they tend to become very productive. It is better to make no evaluative remarks and only write down what children dictate than to give disrupting remarks of approval and encouragement.

In discussing what he calls the "slow gifted child" who is culturally deprived, Riessman (1962) cautions against misinterpreting periods of hesitation and points out that many of these children are better at doing and seeing than at talking and hearing. They often appear to achieve better on performance tests than on verbal tests. They like to draw, and role-playing is an effective technique with them. They appear to think in spatial terms rather than temporal terms and often have poor time perspective. Riessman also recommends the games format for use with the slow gifted child. He points out that Davis and Eells capitalized on this idea in the development of an intelligence test in the form of a game for use with underprivileged children.

NEED FOR A CLOSER LOOK

With kindergarteners or adults nothing can take the place of personal observation. Children enjoy using magnifying glasses. The closer look that it gives them opens up new wonders. The child will be satisfied to watch from a distance at first. This look from a distance, however, does not satisfy his curiosity. Thinking and learning are driven off course when children have no opportunities for a closer look, when they are forbidden to touch, when there is no real chance to encounter all of the exciting things about them.

We place many restrictions on the child's manipulativeness and curiosity. We discourage him by telling him that "curiosity killed the cat." If we were honest we would admit that curiosity makes a "good cat" and that cats are extremely skilled in testing the limits and determining what is safe and what is dangerous. Apparently children, as well as cats, have an irresistible tendency to manipulate and explore objects and this very tendency seems to be the basis for the curiosity and inventiveness of adults. Even in testing situations we find that children who do the most manipulating of objects produce the most ideas and the largest number of original ideas.

Need for Props and Resources

Since learning creatively involves manipulation, experimentation, and what seems to be play, it is natural that children need props and resources both to "warm them up" psychologically and to provide the means for carrying out their ideas. Teachers of gifted children should recognize that parents as well as men in business and industry will supply large quantities of wonderful materials, when they understand the need for them. Often these materials would otherwise be wasted or destroyed. Communities too will provide many of these resources once the need and value are explained.

Need to Keep Alive Fantasy

The fantasy of kindergarten children should be kept alive, developed, and guided. Many teachers and parents try hard to eliminate fantasy at the time children enter school in kindergarten or first grade. They do this because they believe that fantasy is unhealthy and fail to recognize that fantasy can be useful even in adult experience. Imaginative role-playing, telling fantastic stories, making unusual drawings, and the like should be considered as normal aspects of a child's thinking.

We are, of course, interested in developing a sound type of creative problem-solving and decision-making. Fantasy must be kept alive until children achieve the kind of intellectual development that makes this type of thinking possible. For some time it is through fantasy that children must do their experimenting and exploring. In a somewhat different way it also has its uses for adults and should never be abandoned completely.

Need for Embodiment of Ideas

Children rise to greater heights in their thinking if the ideas they produce find embodiment in some concrete form. There is much value in the excitement that comes from seeing their ideas take some form. Children take great pride in murals they paint, the inventions they contrive, the poems and stories they tell, the songs they make up and sing. When children find that others appreciate their productions, they take courage and are eager to keep building onto their ideas, improving them, creating new works, letting one thing lead to others.

Summary

Let us summarize now some of the things the author has learned from kindergarteners about the teaching of gifted children. The gifted kindergartener can become completely absorbed in a task and the passage of time means little to him. The more imaginative he is, the longer he can sit still. Under reasonably favorable conditions he will not flit from one interest to another; he will follow through and try to get at the truth of the matter. He prefers creative ways of learning and has mastered many of the techniques of learning in these ways. Learning by authority does not come naturally to him.

We can be prepared for the lightning quickness of the thinking of kindergarten children, but there are times when we must wait and not interrupt his thought processes by undue intrusion. Primary children quite naturally experiment with looking at things in a different way or at closer range. These tendencies can be reinforced and directed so as to improve his creative behavior. There are times when it is desirable to postpone, at least briefly, learning by authority so that necessary experimentation can take place. In talking with children, it frequently pays to tolerate moments of silence and hesitation to allow time for answers to our questions. Children characteristically begin by looking at things from a distance but are not satisfied until they are able to take a closer look. They also need props and resources for carrying out their ideas and some way in which their ideas can find embodiment in concrete form. Preschoolers prize their individuality and resist efforts to coerce them into being like everybody else. Finally a basic essential is a relationship characterized by affection and a willingness to accompany the child along untraveled pathways.

7

Helping Gifted Children
Become Creative Readers

EVEN creatively gifted children need help in becoming creative readers. Children not creatively gifted but gifted in other ways may need a great deal of help in becoming creative readers. Children who have been overtrained in becoming critical readers or in reading to absorb and remember all of the facts may have difficulty in becoming creative readers. It takes effort and practice to shift from critical or retention reading to creative reading. Then after a child begins reading creatively, there are a number of skills that need further development. In this chapter some of these skills will be identified and ways for developing them will be outlined. The kind of reading involved here may include not only basic readers, literature books, and outside readings but also readings in history, geography, science, mathematics, and other subjects. All fields can provide experiences in creative thinking.

WHY READING CREATIVELY IS IMPORTANT

Even in giving children a realistic view of the world through their reading, it is necessary that they read creatively. Only this way can they grasp the sights, sounds, smells, and tactile sensations of the world. Only by using the imagination can the movements and actions of the world become real. Only if they are read creatively can books become a source of thinking materials in solving problems and coping with life's stresses. Only the creative reader is able to ferret out the truth from what he reads. It takes a creative reader to remember in a meaningful way what is read. Almost all courses in memory improvement make a special point of calling imagination into play.

Besides its use in acquiring a realistic view of the world, reading should be a source of materials for use in solving problems. One's ability to think is limited primarily by his personal experiences and the uses he makes of them in problem solving, in abstracting and generalizing, in judging, and in making decisions. The creative reader increases his store of personal experiences through his reading because he uses the ideas gained as he would firsthand experiences. In solving problems and reaching decisions he is as likely to see the relevance of a story situation or biographical account as he is the relevance of a firsthand experience. What he reads becomes real to him and he can use it.

Ferreting out the truth from what one reads requires that one be both a critical and creative reader. Being a critical reader only makes a child aware of the biases and deficiencies in the accounts of writers. It takes a creative reader to understand the reasons behind discrepant accounts and reach sound conclusions about what is true.

It is apparently not the amount of information one possesses that enables him to think creatively, solve problems, and reach sound decisions, but rather the way he has stored his information and the attitude he has toward it.

What it Means to Read Creatively

In a number of experiments the author has tried to describe some of the essentials of reading creatively. For example, the following instructions were given in an experiment involving the use of different reading sets in mastering textbook assignments (Torrance and Harmon, 1961):

When you read, it is important that you think about the many possible uses of the information which you are reading. It is especially important that you think of the various ways in which the information could be used in your personal and professional life. In reading, do not just ask, "What is the author saying?" Also ask, "How can I use what the author is saying?" Do not stop with just one use. Think of as many uses as you can of the important ideas presented. Jot down some of their uses for future reference or action. It may take some practice before you are really successful in assuming this set or attitude towards your reading, but do not be discouraged. By the third day, you should find it easy to assume this set.

The results of this study indicated rather clearly that the way in which information is stored makes a great deal of difference in how it will be used. The reader might want to practice this set, or attitude, in reading the remainder of this chapter or some other reading assignment.

In the experiment involving the critical and creative reading of research reports, those reading the reports with a critical set were required to describe the defects in the statement of the problem and its importance, the underlying assumptions and hypotheses studied, procedures for collecting and analyzing data, the conclusions and interpretations of the findings, and a critical appraisal of the worth of the research. The creative readers were asked to think of new possibilities suggested by the statement of the problem, other possible hypotheses related to the problem and its solution, improvements which could have been made in collecting and analyzing the data, other possible conclusions and interpretations of the findings, and an appraisal of the possibilities stemming from the findings. In projects given after this experience, students who had read the research reports creatively produced new ideas of their own which were judged to be more creative than were those of their peers who read critically.

There are a number of ways to describe what happens when a person reads creatively. One way is through the use of the definition the author has proposed for creativity: When a person reads creatively, he is sensitive to problems and possibilities in whatever he reads. He makes himself aware of the gaps in knowledge, the unsolved problems, the missing elements, things that are incomplete or out of focus. To resolve this tension, so important in the creative thinking process, the creative reader sees new relationships, creates new combinations, synthesizes relatively unrelated elements into a coherent whole, redefines or transforms certain pieces of information to discover new uses, and builds onto what is known. In this search for solutions he produces a large number of possibilities, uses a great variety of strategies or approaches, looks at the available information in a variety of ways, breaks away from commonplace solutions into bold new ways, and develops his idea by filling in the details and making the idea attractive and exciting to others.

In order for these things to happen in the process of reading, one must be open to his experiences and reflect upon what he reads, discovering relationships among the ideas presented, evaluating them in the light of his experiences. He must be able to play with the possibility that the new idea might be useful and try to envision what its consequences might be. Thus the new idea becomes a center of vivid, concrete images and feeling reactions. He has an inquiring attitude about what he reads. Frequently he tries to identify with the author so that he can grasp what the author had in mind, so that he can predict what the author is going to say next.

How Creative Readers Develop

Teachers can help children become creative readers in two major ways. First they can do things to help heighten the child's expectations and anticipation as a reading task is approached. Second they can permit or encourage children to do something with what is read, either at the time it is being read or afterwards.

HEIGHTENING EXPECTATION AND ANTICIPATION

The creative process itself embodies the tension of anticipation or expectation, and individuals who distinguish themselves in artistic, scientific, and entrepreneurial creation exemplify this tension quite vividly. It has variously been described as the warming up process, the ability to rise to the occasion, or attraction to the unknown, the strange, and the puzzling.

Teachers of gifted children will be able to think of materials and methods for heightening the tension of expectation from kindergarten through graduate school. A few examples of such materials and methods will be offered.

One of the author's favorite sets of material at the preschool and primary levels is a series of books by Bruno Munari, an Italian artist and storyteller; they include *Who's There? Open the Door* (1957), *The Elephant's Wish* (1959), and *The Birthday Present* (1959). *The Elephant's Wish* is especially useful in developing imaginatively the concept and skills of empathy. The story begins: "The elephant is bored with being a big heavy animal. He wishes he could be something else. What do you think he would like to be?" This starts the empathic guessing game. The child is asked to look into the mind of the elephant, imaginatively to put himself in the place of the elephant, and think what he would do if he were tired of being an elephant. Then he is given a look into the elephant's mind by the artist-author through the clever device of a flap on the elephants head, which can be pulled back. "He wishes he could be a little bird who flies and sings." The bird, however, has his problems. "The little bird is bored with flying and singing. He is wishing too. What does he wish?" After some guessing on his part, the child can be given a look into the bird's mind. The story continues with the fish, a lizard, and a fat, lazy ox. The ox wants to be an elephant, illustrating the need for reacting to limitations creatively rather than cynically and using whatever abilities and resources we have.

Somewhat the same effect can be obtained when reading new material in the primary and intermediate grades by asking, before you turn the page in the middle of a story, "What do you think will happen now?" Later you can encourage children to ask questions that will lead them to find relationships among certain facts and thus come to a logical conclusion. This same technique can be used in history, geography, and science. Children can be given enough facts to enable them to make predictions and then asked to make guesses about the consequences. Later they can check their guesses against documentary sources or established facts and try to determine wherein their theorizing went wrong.

We have used this technique in some of the experimental materials created and tested in the fourth grade. In these materials the atmosphere of expectation is created through brief dramas of great moments of scientific and geographical discovery and historical achievement, as well as fantasies. An example from the fantasy series is our use of the famous Italian story *Giovanni and the Giant* (Cunnington, Buckland, and Peterson, 1962). In the dramatization the tape recorder is stopped each time Giovanni gets himself into a predicament. The pupils are asked to think of as many solutions as possible for extricating Giovanni. By the time the tape is completed, each pupil has

enough material for another version of the story. After this kind
of experience pupils may also be invited to expand the story or
put it into a here-and-now setting. Or they may be invited to
write newspaper articles dealing with selected parts of the story
from an "I-was-there" viewpoint. This, in turn, might lead to
reading creatively more material about twelfth-century Italy, the
Crusades, city-states, and the like.

In the intermediate grades and in the high-school years
something of the same effect can be achieved by giving the title
of a book and asking students to guess what the book is about.
Josephine Shotka (1961) has suggested a list of questions which
can be used to stimulate creative reading. They are designed for
stories but can be adapted to biographies, history, and other
kinds of reading materials. Here are some of the questions she
suggests for use before the story is read:

> From the name of the story, what do you think it will be like?
> What experiences do you think the characters will have?
> Do you think this will be a funny story, a sad story, a make-be-
> lieve story, or an exciting story? Why?
> What do you think the characters will be like?

The following is a sample of the questions she suggests for use
during the reading of the story:

> Where does our story take place?
> Have you ever been in a place like this?
> Who are the characters and what kind of persons are they?
> Have you ever met a person like the character in the story?

For use after the reading of the story, she suggests such questions as the following:

> Why did you like or dislike the story?
> What would you have done if you were in the same position as
> the character or characters of the story?
> How do you think the character or characters felt? Have you ever
> felt like this?

The use of such questions emphasizes the fact that reading
creatively involves reactions to the reading material before, during, and after the actual reading. Then there is still the matter of
doing something further with what has been read. One of the
major problems in arousing anticipation and expectation is to

lead the reader to see the fundamental relationships among the facts, ideas, and events that constitute the reading material and between them and the experiences and problems of the reader.

DOING SOMETHING WITH WHAT IS READ

The author was amazed a few years ago when he began giving examinations that require that students do something with the theories and research findings they had studied. One device used was to give important research findings and ask students to list all of the educational uses they could think of for these findings. Student after student would come to him and say, "What do you mean by 'uses'? The only thing that I can think of is to tell it to somebody." This experience helped the author begin understanding why courses in education, psychology, and the other behavioral sciences have so little impact on what happens in classrooms. Students were struggling with courses and learning facts they did not intend ever to use. Indeed it had not occurred to them that such information could be useful in any very concrete or real sense! Some ways by which creative readers can be developed by "doing something with what is read" will be outlined now.

1. *Reproducing What Is Read with Imagination.* Even if one's goal is only to "tell it to someone," as in the case of the author's Educational Psychology students, it can and should be done with imagination. If you have difficulty in getting pupils to read orally with imagination, John Ciardi might help you in this task. The author has been fascinated by Ciardi's recording *I Met a Man* by Pathways of Sound, Inc. This recording grew out of Ciardi's attempt to teach his own daughter how to read with meaning and imagination when she was in the first grade. His aim in the recording is to encourage children to put meaning into their reading instead of mouthing the words, whether the mouthing be slowly or rapidly. He encourages the young listener to make poems "sound like the thing happening."

2. *Elaborating What Is Read.* Next to reproducing what is read comes elaborating what is read. There are many ways of elaborating upon what one reads and thus developing creative readers. Durrell and Chambers (1958) predict that "it will probably be found that well-designed exercises in elaborative thinking in reading will produce higher permanent retention and greater availability of knowledge to new situations." One of the most common means of doing this is to have children illustrate what they read. Other media such as music, songs, rhythmic movement, and dramatics can also be used in elaborating what has been read. Also valuable are modifications of what is read: writing a different ending, changing a character in some specific way and seeing what else this would change, expanding upon a certain episode in a story.

Some children who are having difficulty in learning how to read would probably learn to do so, if given experiences in elaborating what is read. An illustrative case is one reported by Miss Joy Alice Holm (Torrance, 1962 pp. 176–7). Bob was a miserable and withdrawn junior-high-school student. As a high-school student he was considered a hopeless case because he could not read. Throughout elementary school Bob's teachers had called him "sweet but dumb." Now he was too miserable to be "sweet." Bob was in Miss Holm's English class and also in her art class. She worked with him on his reading after school, and he illustrated the stories the class read. Miss Holm writes that Bob's illustrations showed that he understood the thoughts and he transformed them into vivid pictures. Since he could neither write about the meaning and details of a poem or story nor talk about them, Miss Holm permitted him to take his tests by illustrating the stories the class had read. Other students were amazed at the depth of meaning he showed them through his illustrations. Finally, after almost a year of illustrating his way through English class and drawing and painting away many of his conflicts, he increased his reading skills and was able to participate again in sports.

There are a number of remarkable facets of Miss Holm's encounter with Bob. She was willing to embark with him on an untrodden path. What teacher would have thought of letting Bob take his English examinations using figural or visual rather than verbal symbols? Most teachers would be afraid that they could not "grade" or "correct" such an examination paper. By "going along" in this unorthodox fashion, a "hopeless case" learned to read and perhaps escape a life of pathological withdrawal.

This example is offered for two reasons. The technique of elaborating what is read through means other than words may be useful in reaching some slow gifted students and enabling them to achieve some of their potentialities. It is also offered because many parents and teachers believe that a child must first be a *good reader* before he can be a creative reader, The author would maintain, however, that a child is not a good reader unless he is also a creative reader.

For the gifted child, however, work in elaborating what is read will have its greatest usefulness in developing the ability to relate the content of reading to previous knowledge, produce illustrations and applications, practice using what has been read, relate what has been read to other fields, and make associations that integrate reading into action. Durrell and Chambers (1958) suggest that elaborative thinking in connection with reading may be better done in groups of various sizes than in either individual or whole-class activities. They also suggest that specific planning or applications are better than remote or academic tasks and that intensive sequential instruction is more effective than occasional or incidental instruction. This is very similar to the author's suggestion for procedures that permit one activity to lead to another, making use of the power of the "warm-up" process in producing readiness for kinds of learning that would otherwise be unlikely.

3. *Transforming and Rearranging What Is Read.* Third in the author's scale of doing something with what is read is the transformation or rearrangement of what is read. Shakespeare's creativity was of this type. It probably never occurred to Shakespeare that a playwright should invent a plot and characters. With all of the great stories in history, science, geography, and government—with all of the myths and fables available, with all of the great biographies—there are plenty of plots and characters waiting to be brought to life in dramas, songs, paintings, murals, and other forms by creative readers. Of course, in bringing these plots and characters to life in

such a way, students will need to read creatively from a number of sources. What results will be a creative recombination and transformation of what has been read.

The book report assignment or report on other outside reading can also be made a transformation of what has been read. Mauree Applegate (1962) and others have given an exciting variety of suggestions for such assignments. The following are some of Applegate's suggestions:

1. What was your favorite character like? Make a drawing and point out passages in the story which make you think this is the way your character looks.

2. Before you read the book, write the story the title makes you think of; then when you read the book, write the report of the real story and chuckle at the difference. (You may feel that you have a better story.)

3. Write an interview between a character in the book and the author, between you and the author, between two characters in the book, between you and a character in the book, or between you and a friend about the book.

4. Write your book report in verse.

5. You have just finished reading a biography. Pretend you visited the person when he was your age. Tell about the fun you had.

6. Choose a lively scene from a book you and your friends have read and either dramatize it or make a puppet play of it.

7. Have a friend interview you about a book of which you pretend to be the author.

8. Make a hand-rolled movie of a book you have read.

9. Make a radio or television play of your favorite book.

Teachers of gifted children will be able to think of many others that are even more exciting than the ones Applegate suggests. With little prodding, gifted children themselves will invent an astounding array of ideas.

4. *Going Beyond What Is Read.* In the creative process one thing must be permitted to lead to another. Creativity begets creativity. A good story is likely to evoke many ideas and questions which can send the reader beyond the story. Going beyond a basic reader story or great literary work is a natural and integral part of all group-directed reading.

It is to be anticipated that there will in the very near future be sets of basal readers and literature books specifically designed to develop creative and critical readers, giving practice in doing something with what has been read.

The idea of permitting one thing to lead to another is the very essence of the experimental materials we have been producing for the fourth grade. Basic to our strategy is generating enthusiasm, interest, and curiosity through the tape-recorded drama and then using this warm-up to get pupils to produce something. They are then encouraged to produce something on the basis of what they have already produced. Additional reading may come in at any one of several stages in the process, and we believe that such reading is almost certain to be creative reading. Let us examine an example from one of the lessons based on *Eyes at Their Fingertips,* the story of Louis Braille (Cunnington, Myers, Buckland, and Peterson, 1962). The instructions for the first step go something like the following:

> One of the big reasons Louis Braille thought of and worked out a way for blind people to read and write better was that the old way really bothered him. It really got under his skin that little blind children had to read out of books that were so big that they couldn't carry them around. And besides, reading raised or embossed writing wasn't very accurate. Try to think of as many things as you can that really bother you and get on your nerves—things that bother you so much that you would like to change them or invent something new to make them less annoying. List as many of them as you can.

Immediately after this list has been produced, we go ahead to the second stage with the following instructions:

> Of all the things you listed, what bothers you most? What really gets you down? Is there any one of the things you listed on the first page that towers over all of the others and makes them seem small? Pick out one of the things you have just listed and write it down.

Then follows:

> Now think of all of the things that you can about this annoyance, or "thorn in your flesh," that make it annoying and list them below. What is there about it that bothers you?

After this pupils are told:

> Now list as many things as you can think of that would make it less annoying or remove the annoyance from your life. It doesn't have to be something that is now possible. Play being a magician and list all of the things that would make it ideal.

After thinking this through, they are asked to continue with the following instructions:

> Now think of something you could invent or some plan that would remove some of the things that bother you about this annoyance and would have as many as possible of the characteristics you just listed.

After this we definitely have a phase that calls for creative reading. The orientation for this is as follows:

Louis Braille was helped in developing his kind of writing because he was familiar with sonography which had proven unsuccessful. Do you know of any unsuccessful attempts to solve the problem you selected? If you do, write them below. If you don't know of any, how could you find out if there have been any?

The next phase is introduced as follows:

If you thought of some unsuccessful attempt to solve your problem, what would have to be changed about it to make it successful?

Following this step pupils are encouraged to draw a picture or diagram of the invention, plan, or procedure they have in mind or to describe it as fully as possible. As a final step they are asked to think of the possible consequences of their invention or plan. This activity is introduced in the following words:

If you were to succeed with your invention or plan, it would change many things. Think of as many things as you can that would probably be changed, if your invention or plan becomes successful.

It will be noted that an effort has been made to reproduce essentially the same thinking process Louis Braille pursued in working out a system of writing and reading for the blind. In each of the great moments of discovery an effort is made to distill in the drama as much as possible the essence of the thinking of the scientist or inventor. Benjamin Franklin's thinking processes were motivated in quite a different way from Braille's. He was sensitive to the needs of other people and he kept inventing and suggesting things that would solve problems for other people—for example, bifocals, lightning rods, coal stoves, mail-delivery service, police and fire departments, political cartoons, Poor Richard sayings, street lights, and the like. Thus, instead of starting with personal concerns with the Benjamin Franklin story, we start children by having them observe what things bother other people. In this way children are brought back again and again to read creatively.

Conclusion

Since most gifted children are avid readers, guidance that will improve their skills as creative readers is especially promising and might influence performance in all areas of the curriculum.

It has been the purpose of this chapter to expand ideas about what it means to read creatively and to suggest some concepts that will be useful in increasing the chances that gifted children will become creative readers. It is up to teachers of gifted children to find ways of heightening expectations and anticipation and invent ways of getting pupils to do something with what has been read.

8

Developing Research Concepts
and Skills

SOME YEARS AGO when the author began talking about his experience in teaching gifted sixth-grade pupils concepts and skills in doing research, most of his colleagues regarded his accounts as fantasy. Even after he and Myers produced a monograph and an article about the 1961 experiences in *Gifted Child Quarterly* (Torrance and Myers, 1962ab), few people took these accounts seriously. As time has passed, he has been reassured by many teachers that his experiences in teaching research concepts and skills to elementary pupils could be replicated by intelligent and imaginative teachers. Other colleagues found the materials contained in the monograph useful in teaching high-school and college undergraduates research concepts and skills. Whenever the author has met the parents of the pupils in these early classes three and four years afterwards, they almost always report spontaneously that their children are still using the research concepts and skills learned in the sixth grade in school and out-of-school activities. Thus, research concepts learned in the sixth grade became tools in future learning and thinking.

Since research has become increasingly complex, it is not strange that people would believe that teaching gifted elementary-school children concepts and skills of doing research is fantasy. The teaching of research concepts and skills has almost always been reserved for the graduate-school period, especially in education. Furthermore there has been a tendency in some graduate schools to eliminate the teaching of research concepts and skills from the first year of graduate work. Discussions on teaching elementary pupils how to do research are usually limited to procedures for "looking something up in the library" and almost never touch upon the methods and concepts of creative scientific research. Textbooks on methods of teaching in high school are seldom much better in this regard.

Promising Developments

Already there are a number of scattered experiences that indicate that gifted elementary and high-school students have a great readiness for research and can achieve very worthwhile results, when given a chance. Quite exciting has been Jablonski's work at the University of Pittsburgh (Guilford, 1962a; Taylor, 1964c). Jablonski discovered the potential of gifted high-school students participating in National Science Foundation Summer Science Programs. He encouraged his summer proteges to continue their research work the year round and solicited the help of personnel in Pittsburgh schools. Some of their experiments have been published in regular professional journals against the competition of mature and experienced scientists. Jablonski estimates that 25 per cent of his high-school researchers are producing publishable material.

Jablonski wanted next to begin working with younger students. His colleagues told him that this was really getting ridiculous, but nevertheless he went ahead with projects with fourth-, fifth-, and sixth-grade students. Jablonski admits that he had grossly underestimated the readiness of these children to do research. Groups of them have joined him in cancer research. They asked the meaning of words and soon mastered the technical language just as if they were learning English. As a result, these youngsters produced useful research ideas and discoveries.

J. Richard Suchman (1961) has developed a system of inquiry training for elementary pupils which represents an attempt to translate ideas concerning this problem into concrete materials, systematic methods, and evaluation instruments and to test them. The program is designed to teach the skills believed to be necessary for effective inquiry. It includes a series of short motion pictures of physics demonstrations which pose problems of cause and effect. Children are shown these films and instructed to find out why the events took place as they did. They ask the teacher questions which can be answered by "yes" or "no." This requires them to think through and organize their questions. Each question involves a concrete hypothesis. When a child thinks he can explain the phenomena, he is permitted to give his explanation. If it is incomplete or incorrect, he is permitted to ask other questions.

Within the framework of Suchman's inquiry training, elementary pupils learn fundamental skills of scientific inquiry. They are not confronted with annoying problems of instrumentation and tedious routines of physical data collection. The project described in this monograph represents an attempt to include the instrumentation and collection or original data in a way that will not be overwhelming. For sometime the author has believed that most research concepts and many research skills can be taught to elementary pupils, especially gifted ones. He has been convinced too that if gifted children can be taught these concepts and skills at an early age, they will have available some very powerful tools to aid them in their learning and thinking from that time onward. This should make learning more exciting and the search for "truth" more rewarding.

Since 1959–60, the author has tested this idea in part through a five-day course taught to the High Achievers Class, a class of carefully selected gifted sixth-graders, at the Riverside Elementary School of Bloomington, Minnesota. Each year the course has been varied. The course as described herein may suggest quite different ideas to different teachers. Some may want to expand the program as developed by the authors others may wish to select from it. The examples of problems and projects should be regarded only as illustrations.

An Illustrative Experience: The Course for Gifted Sixth-Graders

The class with which the course was developed consisted of 46 pupils selected on the basis of achievement and intelligence (minimum Stanford-Binet IQ, 135). Each morning pupils functioned as two separate classes under different teachers. During this period they followed essentially the same curriculum as other sixth-grade classes, except that they had lessons in French. This left the afternoons free for other ventures. On alternate weeks they worked on their "strengths and weaknesses" under the direction of their teachers. During the other weeks both groups studied for a week with "alter teachers"—experts in some special field such as medicine, journalism, art, music, psychology, architecture, politics. The course on "how to do research" was offered as a part of the alter-teacher program.

MAJOR OBJECTIVES OF THE COURSE

The course was presented to the High Achievers Class as one in educational research. Its major objectives were:

1. To familiarize gifted elementary pupils with some of the most powerful concepts of research in the behavioral sciences, in order that these concepts might become tools in their learning early in their educational careers,

2. To communicate to gifted pupils the excitement of doing original research, exploring the unknown and pushing forward knowledge,

3. To provide experiences in participating in educational research and in conducting and reporting experiments with real consequences,

4. To develop in gifted elementary pupils some skills in formulating hypotheses, testing them, and in reporting the results,

5. To aid gifted elementary pupils in the further development of their self-concepts by making them aware of some of their own creative thinking processes and abilities.

LESSON ONE: What Is Research?

The first session began with an exploration of the concept of "research." Some defined it as a "way of digging into things." Others associated "research" with "experimenting" and others with "looking things up in books." Some defined it as a way of "finding out the truth about things that you don't know or nobody knows." Using the materials that had been offered, it was concluded that there are many things we do not know—that no one knows—and that we can find out many of the things we do not know by a more or less formal, systematic, intensive process of carrying on the scientific method.

What's in the Box?[1]

Following this preliminary exploration of the general nature of research, the "What's-in-the-Box" game was used to give the High Achievers an opportunity to develop a concept of the research process through a personal experience. The pupils were shown two boxes. They all agreed that none of them really knew what was in either of the boxes. The two classes were then invited to enter into a contest to see which could find out what was in one of the boxes. Classes returned to their rooms which were just across the hall from one another, one working with the author and the other with R. E. Myers.

In both groups the pupils were told that the object in the box was round. They were then invited to make several wild guesses of round things which might be in the box. They agreed, however, that at this point no one really knew which of the guesses was correct or whether any of them were correct. When asked to find out what was in the box without opening it, they immediately wanted to experiment—to lift the box, shake it, smell it, and otherwise examine it. One group found that the object inside the box made no sound and was quite light. They immediately eliminated all objects that would make a sound or would be heavy. Some said that there was an odor; others could detect no odor. No one could specifically identify the odor.

The other group found that the object in its box made a sound, was light, and was apparently quite small as it rattled around very easily. No one could detect any odor. This group then eliminated soft objects, heavy objects, large objects, and objects having strong odors. Thus they eliminated the kinds of objects the first group had retained and kept the kinds of objects it had eliminated.

After eliminating obviously incorrect hypotheses, each group made new hypotheses, or guesses, and started asking questions which could be answered by "yes" or "no." They eliminated the guesses one by one and finally hit upon the correct identity—in one case, a powder puff, in the other, a Sucret (cough drop). This was then verified by opening the box and examining the object.

[1] The author is indebted to Lawrence Conray, School of Education, University of Michigan, for the "What's in the Box?" idea for teaching multiple hypothesis-making and related concepts.

The persons who identified the objects correctly then described the process of *synthesis* by which they arrived at the correct answer. Others described the process by which they had arrived at incorrect guesses near the end of the process and tried to identify what they thought had "thrown them off."

In summarizing the experience, the class identified the following steps in the process:

1. Recognizing that you don't know something.
2. Making wild guesses (multiple hypotheses) on the basis of available information (general appearance).
3. Closer examination and observation, experimenting, testing.
4. Eliminating obviously incorrect guesses on basis of additional information.
5. Making "better guesses in the light of new information.
6. Asking questions to test guesses (hypotheses).
7. Eliminating incorrect guesses on basis of additional information.
8. Making "closer" guesses, synthesizing accumulated information.
9. Verifying final answer.

At each step, an effort was made to relate the experiences of group members to research concepts.

Three Kinds of Research

After drawing conclusions concerning the steps in the process of research, they were told that these steps might be carried out in any one of three kinds of research: historical, descriptive, and experimental. Each type was discussed briefly.

LESSON TWO: An Experience in Historiography

A Personal Problem in Historical Research

An attempt was made to lay a beginning for the development of the concepts of historical research through the use of a personal problem. Near the end of the first session the High Achievers were given the first of the "How-Did-You-Grow?" exercises (Appendix B). They were asked to make guesses, or estimates, concerning the trends in their development from first through sixth grade in the following eight characteristics, in the form of developmental curves:

shoe size;
height;
curiosity;
reading speed;
imagination;
spelling;
independence in thinking;
arithmetic computation.

Each pupil was given a set of the same charts they had just filled out and told to collect all of the data they could to test the trends they had already hypothesized. Before trying to recall specific information or to collect any information, they were asked to list on the booklet all of the ways they could think of to check their guesses. Some of these were discussed briefly. They were also asked to record what information they could recall or collect relevant to each of the eight aspects of development.

The Experience in Historical Research

The next day, the High Achievers reported a great variety of sources of information used in trying to establish their developmental curves more accurately. They discovered that these sources could be classified either as "records" or as "witnesses."

The experiences were related to the concepts of historical research. One of the first problems introduced by them was that of "bias." They asked, "What do you do when witnesses tell you just the opposite?" This was identified as the problem of "bias." Several indicated that their mothers had said that they were very curious when they were young but that they had become less curious as they grew older. Their fathers, however, said that they had shown little evidence of curiosity until the past two or three years. They were then asked to think of the kinds of observations their mothers might have made and of the kinds of observations their fathers might have made. From this they were able to formulate several hypotheses concerning the reasons for the discrepancies in the conclusions of their mothers and fathers. Apparently mothers have more contacts with their children during their early years than do fathers and are naturally more aware of their curiosity tendencies. As mothers gradually discourage their question asking, become unable or refuse to answer their questions, children turn increasingly to their fathers.

The "frame of reference" was also a frequent problem. In a number of instances many made their estimates in quantitative terms such as shoe size, feet and inches, words per minute, spelling words added, and the like. Some established their frame of reference in terms of their peers; others did year-by-year comparisons with themselves.

LESSON THREE: An Experience in Descriptive Research

To generate a set of data for use in a descriptive study, the High Achievers were administered the Ask-and-Guess Test. A Mother Goose print of Mother Hubbard was used as the stimulus material. The print shows Mother Hubbard opening the cupboard which is completely bare and the dog looking at the empty cupboard. The following general orientation was given for the task:

One good way of finding out things that we don't know is to ask questions. To get the information we want, we have to ask the right questions. Sometimes we can't find out by asking questions, so we have to make the best guesses we can. Then, whenever we can, we try to find out if our guesses are correct. The three tasks which we shall do now will give you a chance to show how good you are at asking questions and making guesses to find out things.

They were first instructed to produce as many questions as they could think of concerning the events depicted. Next they were asked to formulate hypotheses about the possible causes of the events and finally they were asked to formulate hypotheses about possible consequences.

Upon completion of the Ask-and-Guess Test, the High Achievers were confronted with the problem of devising ways of quantifying and describing their performance on the three tasks they had just completed. They decided that one way to describe their performance would be to count the number of questions, causes, and consequences produced. They were asked then to do this. In counting the number of questions asked, they were cautioned not to count any questions that could have been answered by looking at the picture. In the case of "causes" they were asked to check to see if each response made some hypothesis about causation and to eliminate responses that were merely sequences of events that might have occurred before the action. In the case of "consequences" the same type of check was suggested.

They decided that one way to describe the group would be to add the number of responses to each of the parts for all of the class and divide it by the number who took the test. They were told that this was known in statistics as the "mean" and was a "measure of central tendency." They were asked how else we might describe some central tendency of the group. Someone suggested that the score of the middle ranked person might be used. The instructor identified this as the "median." They were also told that another useful way of describing a group is to determine the typical or "modal," performance, the score made by the largest number of people. They were then asked to determine the mean, median, and mode of their own scores which had been placed on the blackboard.

Someone suggested that the highest and lowest scores would also help in describing their performance and noted that scores on the "Ask" part ran from 5 to 19, "Causes" from 0 to 17, "Consequences" from 5 to 22, and total scores from 14 to 51. This was identified as the "range," a measure of the way in which they vary. (Since the data as arranged did not suggest a clear illustration of other measures of variability, no effort was made at this point to develop further the concepts of variance, standard deviation, and the like.)

In the above procedure, the following statistical notations were introduced:

$$\Sigma X = \text{sum of the numbers}$$
$$N = \text{number of scores}$$
$$X = \text{mean}$$

It was then suggested that they might describe their performance more completely and meaningfully by comparisons within their own group and between their group and some other groups. They then obtained the means and medians for boys and girls separately. It was noted that both the means and medians for the girls were higher than those of the boys on all three scores and the total. They were then confronted with the problem of whether the differences are great enough to be accepted with confidence or if they might have occurred by chance. Some did not believe that the differences were large enough to amount to anything and that boys might do as well or better than girls, if given the same or a similar task. They were then introduced to the concept of levels of confidence and the use of the t test to determine the level of confidence of differences in means.

Tests of significance were made by the author and reported to the class the next day, all three being significant at better than the 5 per cent level.

It was pointed out that comparing a group with some other groups is an aid in describing performance. As a matter of interest, the following comparative data were compiled from other studies:

| | | Means | | |
Comparison Group	Questions	Causes	Conseq.	Totals
High Achievers	10.86	8.45	12.52	31.84
Regular sixth grade in suburban school	7.59	4.70	5.30	17.59
Twelfth grade at University High School	10.38	7.24	10.34	27.96
Graduate students in Educational Psychology 159	13.35	8.71	11.40	33.46
Nursing students, Seniors	10.80	8.07	9.60	28.47

It was apparent from these data that the High Achievers performed considerably better than a regular sixth grade class in the area, as well or better than twelfth-grade students at University High School and nursing students at a local diploma school, and almost as well as graduate students in the author's class in Educational Psychology (Personality Development and Mental Hygiene). It was cautioned, however, that we would have to compute tests of significance before we could determine the confidence to be placed in the observed differences.

Time did not permit the development of the concept of variability as thoroughly in the present course as in the earlier ones. In earlier courses, scores on the *Things Done Check List*, a list of 243 science activities, were used as the basis for developing concepts of descriptive statistics. With these data the concept of variance is more obvious and is usually grasped spontaneously. Someone noted, "Boys are more variable in the number of activities they checked. See, some of the boys are higher than any of the girls and some of them are lower than any of the girls. The girls are in a kind of narrow band."

Teachers who have had no training in statistics probably should not attempt to develop the statistical concepts. For teachers who require some review of statistical concepts simplified guides are available. No emphasis was placed upon the achievement of skills in computing the statistics; a longer allotment of time would have been necessary. With a little instruction, however, there is no reason why pupils cannot compute means, tests of significance, and standard deviations. The present author believes, however, that the important thing is that gifted children grasp the concepts, and they do this readily. Actually this should not be hard to understand. Most of them are achieving at about the tenth- or eleventh-grade level in reading and other general educational skills. In the comparative data given in this chapter, it will be noted that their performance on causal and consequential hypotheses approaches that of graduate students in educational psychology.

LESSON FOUR: An Experience in Quantification

The dependence of research upon quantification, or measurement, was discussed briefly. It was pointed out that scientific advances in some areas are blocked until problems of measurement can be solved. When measurement problems are solved, there is frequently a flood of research, and rapid progress in the field follows. Examples of of quantification were pointed out in the historical and descriptive studies already conducted.

Since the High Achievers had been assigned to write an imaginative story for their homework, the problem of quantifying their stories was considered. The stories assigned for this purpose concerned animals and persons with divergent characteristics, such as *The Lion That Would Not Roar, The Flying Monkey, The Man Who Cries*, and the like.

Quantification of Stories

It was pointed out that some of the characteristics of their stories were easy to quantify objectively, but that others would require more thinking. They readily listed those that could be quantified objectively. These included:

> number of words;
> number of sentences;
> number of paragraphs;
> number writing on each topic;
> number who made up their own topics;
> amount of time required to write the stories;
> number of words misspelled and percentage of words misspelled;
> number of errors in punctuation;
> number of errors in capitalization;
> number of action words;
> number having happy endings.

It was agreed that once numbers had been assigned to these characteristics, we could then apply concepts such as mean, median, mode, range, and the like.

The class was then asked to identify other qualities of stories that might be useful in describing their stories or testing hypotheses about them. They then concluded that it would be valuable if we could quantify the "interest" the stories generated in the reader, their originality, and their content.

Concerning the quantification of "interest," the class suggested that consideration be given to such things as the use of surprise, humor, the personal element, and the like. Similarly they discussed signs that might be used in quantifying "originality." They suggested such things as unusual solution or ending, surprise, unusual setting or plot, invented words or names, picturesque or colorful words or expressions, and the like. It was suggested that a story could be checked for the absence or presence of these qualities and a rough measure or estimate could be determined thereby.

Attention was then turned to the analysis of content. Since all of the stories involved some divergent characteristic of an animal or person, it was then suggested that we might center our analysis on the handling of the divergent characteristic (what made them different). Since the author had developed such a system (Torrance, 1964a), categories already developed were used so that the High Achievers could compare their stories with those written by children in other countries. They were shown stories written on the same topics by children in India, Turkey, Greece, France, and Germany. They were then shown how they could compare the characteristics of their stories with those of children in the other countries. Again the problem of significant differences was discussed and the concept of chi square introduced. They were then taught how to use a nomograph for determining the significance of the difference between percentages.

LESSON FIVE: An Experience in Experimental Research

To provide an experience in experimental research and to develop an understanding of additional research concepts, the High Achievers served as subjects of an experiment on the effects of differential rewards upon various kinds of creative thinking. The general hypothesis upon which the experiment was based is that pupils tend to achieve along whatever lines they are rewarded.

Procedure

The two classrooms were each divided randomly into Groups A and B. This was done by having each pupil draw an assignment card from a stack which had been carefully and obviously shuffled. The two experimenters tossed a coin to see who would have which group and who would handle which treatment. (These arrangements were made rather obvious to communicate the concepts of randomization of treatments and the like. Afterwards the reasons for them were explained.) All A's assembled in one room and all B's in the other.

Group A was given the following instructions:

Your task is to think of ideas for improving this stuffed toy dog so that it will be more fun for a child to play with. Try to think of as many ideas as you can. Don't worry about how good your ideas are or how much it would cost to carry them out. A prize of two dollars will be awarded to the one who thinks of the largest number of ideas, regardless of how clever or original they are. Of course you want to think of clever and original ideas, so we shall give a prize of twenty-five cents to the one who thinks of the largest number of unusual or original ideas. You will have only ten minutes, so you will want to make good use of your time.

Group B was shown identically the same stuffed toy dog and given essentially the same instructions, except that the rewards for originality and fluency were reversed.

Responses were scored for fluency, flexibility, and originality. Fluency was determined by counting the number of relevant ideas given. Ideas not related to the improvement of the toy as something to play with were eliminated. Flexibility was determined by counting the number of different approaches used in making the improvements (Torrance, 1962a). A response was scored as original if it were given by fewer than 5 per cent of the subjects in a norm population of 600 subjects and if it showed creative strength (were not obvious).

Reporting Results

The results of the experiment were reported to the class on the following day, as shown in Table 1.

TABLE 1

Means, Standard Deviations, and Tests of Significance of Differences of Mean Fluency, Flexibility, and Originality Scores under Two Conditions

Score and Condition	Number	Mean	Standard Deviation	t-Ratio	Probability
Fluency, condition A	23	23.0	7.95		
Fluency, condition B	22	20.4	6.73	1.19	<.25
Flexibility, condition A	23	8.5	2.43		
Flexibility, condition B	22	8.5	1.84	0.00	—
Originality, condition A	23	6.2	3.60		
Originality, condition B	22	12.2	6.12	4.00	<.001

These results provided an excellent opportunity to illustrate the concept of level of confidence, since each of the three results can be accepted at different levels of confidence. The difference in originality can be accepted with a high level of confidence. We can have little confidence in the difference in fluency, and there is no difference at all in flexibility. The results suggest that rewarding originality in thinking does in fact increase the originality of the ideas produced without greatly affecting the number of ideas produced.

The results also provide data for showing that some experimental treatments produce greater variability or are more erratic in their effects than others. Under the conditions of the present experiment rewarding originality produces greater variability in originality scores than does rewarding fluency. (The difference is statistically significant at the 5 per cent level of confidence.)

The results were presented to the class in graphic form also, both to communicate the results more effectively and to give the class another model for use in presenting data.

LESSON SIX: An Experiment of Their Own

The climax of the course was an experiment conducted by the High Achievers themselves in the third, fourth, and fifth grades. Experience had shown that it was not desirable to have them conduct experiments in the other sixth grade classes.

The Pilot Study

To give them experience in dealing with the materials of the experiment, a pilot study was conducted with the High Achievers as subjects. They were given the following Horse-Trading Problem:

You bought a horse for $60 and sold it for $70. You then decided that you wanted the horse back. You had to pay $80 for it this time but you sold it again for $90. How did you come out in all of this trading? Did you make or lose any money? How much did you gain or lose, if any?

When asked for their responses, the following results were obtained:

19 said that he would gain $10.
14 said that he would break even.
6 said that he would make $20.

No one said that he would gain $30, until the experimenter asked those who had not held up their hands if they had gotten $30 (the least frequent incorrect answer in most groups tested by the author). After this several of those who had reported other answers shifted to $30. After the correct answer ($20) had been given and discussed, it was noted that some of them were uncertain of their answers and were willing to shift to an incorrect answer.

The High Achievers were then given the instructions for conducting the experiment. The class was divided into ten research teams, given the materials they would need to conduct the experiment (step-by-step procedures for experiment, answer cards, and retest questionnaires), and assigned classrooms for the conduct of the experiment the following morning. On the following day they were given some more tools for analyzing their data to describe and draw inferences concerning the problem being studied. They were given practice in converting proportions to per cents, using the nomograph to determine the level of confidence of differences in per cents, making bar graphs, and the like. They were also given the following dittoed outline to guide them in preparing their reports:

One important aspect of the research process is the communication of your results to others. When we find out something, we want to tell others about it. A good research report should tell the following five things:

1. THE PURPOSE OF THE STUDY: Why did you perform the study? What was it that you didn't know? What were you trying to find out?

2. PROCEDURES: What was done? Who performed the experiment? What materials did they use? Who were the subjects? How many were there? What did the experimenter do and what did the subjects do? These things should be described in such a way that someone else could carry out the study and expect to obtain the same results.

3. RESULTS: What happened? What did you find out? This should include a presentation of your data in tables, charts, or the like.

4. DISCUSSION: What do your results mean? Try to explain your findings and their meaning.

5. CONCLUSIONS: What does it all add up to? What can you be reasonably certain about? How certain can you be?

The Reports

Each of the ten research teams brought its completed report to the last meeting of the class. Almost all of the reports were well-organized and were written in good form. It was evident from most of the reports that the writing had been a team effort, each making a contribution. The reports did not contain as many new hypotheses as did reports of the previous year when more emphasis has been placed on hypothesis making and the importance of serendipity.

Findings from the Total Study

One by-product of teaching gifted children research skills and concepts is the contribution experiments conducted in such settings make to the development and testing of new hypotheses. As already shown, the historical research project yielded a number of hypotheses which had not occurred previously to the author. The experiment conducted by the children helped plot in a new way the increase in peer influence and the decline in adult influence in searching for solutions to problems. These results were later replicated in two other schools by experienced researchers and will be reported in forthcoming articles.

No attempt was made to make a comprehensive evaluation of the outcomes of this one-week course on research. Three sets of evidence, however, provide at least a tentative evaluation of some of the outcomes of this set of experiences. A brief inventory test administered during the last twenty minutes of the course indicated that some of the High Achievers had mastered almost all of the concepts and that a majority of them had mastered all except five of the 43 concepts included in the test. Certain experiences during the week indicated that the teachers had modified the way in which they perceived some of their pupils' potentialities. Follow-up discussions with the principal, teachers, and pupils five months later indicated that many of the concepts and skills introduced were used throughout the remainder of the term in a variety of ways in all areas of the curriculum.

9

Becoming a Teacher of Gifted Children

ONE'S TEACHING A UNIQUE INVENTION

THE PROCESS of becoming a teacher of gifted children is much like the process of creative thinking itself. If you are counting upon your college education, your courses in education, or your student teaching to "make" you a teacher, you will be disappointed. You might learn much about the subjects you will be teaching, the nature of children, the learning process, the methods and materials of instruction, and the like, but this is not enough. In this book an effort has been made to acquaint you with the most forward-looking information available concerning the nature of giftedness, the goals of educating gifted children, ways of identifying and motivating them, and examples of how you can help them establish a sound foundation for continued development, develop as creative readers, and acquire some of the concepts and skills of investigation. All of these things are inadequate. They must be combined with your own potentialities and the needs of your own pupils in such a way as to become your own unique invention, your way of teaching. This unique invention of the teacher is tremendously important in the teaching of gifted children to help them discover and become their potentialities.

The teacher's invention emerges through the creative process of trying to accomplish some goal. As you fail or succeed in your teaching goals, you become aware of your deficiencies, defects in your techniques and strategies, and gaps in your knowledge. You draw upon your past experiences and increase your search for clues in your ongoing experiences. You try to apply creatively the scientifically developed principles learned in your professional education or through your reading. Then you read and study and puzzle some more. You see things of which you have hitherto been unaware. You make guesses, or formulate hypotheses, concerning the solution. You test and modify these hypotheses and tell others what you have discovered. Through the pain and ecstasy that accompany this process, your personal invention occurs!

Since your way of teaching must be your own invention, no one can present you with a prescription for creating the conditions most favorable for the release of creativity. Your own personality resources and needs, your intellectual resources and skills, the needs and abilities of your pupils, and the expectations of the community in which you are teaching all interact to determine the most effective methods and materials. It *is* possible, however, to derive from experience and research some general principles which increase markedly the chances that your teaching will release the potential of gifted children. It is possible to create teaching methods and instructional materials that have built into them many tested principles. It is the teacher's creative task to weave all of them into new combinations that meet the needs and abilities of his pupils and is in harmony with the needs and abilities of the teacher.

Major Requirements of the Teacher's Invention

Frequently inventors and scientific discoverers have found their tasks easy as soon as they were able to define the characteristics or requirements of the invention or the object of their search. We can do this to a certain extent in regard to becoming a teacher of gifted children. It seems rather certain in the light of the concepts of giftedness presented in this book that teaching gifted children requires the most sensitive and alert kind of guidance and direction possible. It requires a most receptive type of listening, seeing, and feeling. The teacher of gifted children should himself be fully alive, well educated, curious and excited about learning, and free of hostility and the pathological need to punish. He must be prepared to permit one thing to lead to another and in some cases to become the sponsor or patron of gifted children—or help them find someone else who can fill this role.

It is common for teachers to talk about the forces in their environment that inhibit them in realizing their potentialities as teachers. Certainly there are in our society and in our systems of education many forces that threaten the teacher's individuality and cause him to conform to behavioral norms. Let us take a look at some of the more common forces within ourselves that inhibit us in our search for our unique invention, our way of teaching.

RANDOM THINKING RATHER THAN ABSORBED THINKING

In achieving your unique invention, your way of teaching, there are times when you will need to give your mind completely to the problem. Some people incorrectly associate invention and discovery with a random, aimless kind of behavior. It is true that many great ideas seem to occur when a person is relaxed—while sitting in the bathtub, during church services, or while shaving. Unfailingly, however, such occurrences were preceded by periods of concentrated attention during which the mind had been wholly occupied with the problem.

NO TIME FOR THINKING AND DAYDREAMING

Absorbed thinking takes time. The clock is indeed a tyrant, but much can be done to soften its tyranny. One of the first things we have to do is get over the Puritanical compulsion to look busy and decide to make thinking a legitimate acitivity. Do not be afraid to leave a part of your day unscheduled with activities in which you appear to be busy, do not be afraid to daydream occasionally, and do not be ashamed if someone catches you occasionally doing something in an absentminded manner.

LACK OF INTELLECTUAL HONESTY

We frequently fear being honest lest someone ridicule or derogate our ideas. We have been conditioned in so many ways to be less than honest, narcotizing our creative functioning. We desire to appear to be rather than really be. In achieving your unique way of teaching, you will want to free yourself of all encumbrances that hinder you in your work, all beliefs that are false, all conventions and forms that are cramping, and all duties other than those that help you and your pupils achieve your potentialities.

THE UNPREPARED MIND

Some people believe that the more you know, the less likely you are to produce inventions and discoveries. This is a false belief, however. "Chance favors the prepared mind," as Louis Pasteur said. We do encounter an interesting paradox on this point, however. Familiarity with existing knowledge is necessary for the achievement of new knowledge, yet the existence of prior knowledge about a problem hinders the possibilities of the achievement of new knowledge. Preconceptions are often blamed for missed discoveries. As pointed out in the chapter on creative reading, much depends upon the attitude we have toward the knowledge we possess.

FAILURE TO INVESTIGATE AND EXPLORE

Even studies of awareness and perception indicate that skills in these areas are dependent upon opportunities to investigate, explore, and examine the detailed nature of objects, situations, and ideas. In the life of the teacher of gifted children there should never be any period when the process of experimentation and testing ceases.

FAILURE TO INVESTIGATE THINGS ANEW AND IN DEPTH

Students in education frequently complain about repetition and emphasis on the commonplace and obvious. This is because they—and their teachers—have not mastered the skills of looking at things anew and in greater depth. From studies of perception, however, it is clear that the meaning and grasp of an object change as we shift our point of observation. Details previously missed may become extremely important. After changing a goal or obtaining additional information, the meaning of something familiar may also change. Many inventions and discoveries (Gordon, 1961) occur through deliberate methods of making the familiar strange or unfamiliar.

IMPOVERISHED STORE OF IMAGERY

A person will have difficulty in thinking creatively if he lacks a rich store of imagery. A well-filled storehouse of imagery will be useful to the teacher of gifted children in search for his invention. One way of enriching one's imagery is through developing a keen awareness of the environment by experiencing it in detail, by getting a variety of sensory experiences, through first-hand experiences, through empathizing and identifying with others, by becoming involved in life. Another way is through the world's literature.

FAILURE TO RECORD IDEAS

Sometimes we feel rather devoid of ideas until we start recording them. We frequently fail to hold onto ideas because they occur at some of the funniest times and places and we fail to "capture" them. Even children can be motivated to cultivate the idea-trap habit of jotting down ideas for future use and developing them when the opportunity arises.

FEAR OF INDIVIDUALITY

It is difficult for us to free ourselves from other people's "should's." We are so afraid that we are going to hurt someone's feelings or that someone is not going to like us that we make compromises which hurt both ourselves and others, reducing severely our potentialities. Very few truly creative people who have made outstanding contributions to society have been popular and well liked in their day. In fact many of them have been hated. The truly creative person has something urgent to say and constantly seeks new aspects of the truth.

FAILURE TO BE ONESELF

Perhaps the most important word of counsel for the teacher of gifted children in becoming his potentialities as a teacher is that old truism, "Be yourself if you want to contribute anything original and worthwhile." Such advice is difficult to take because we are hampered by pretense and diffidence, self-doubts and lack of stable anchors, and confused self-concepts. Know the value of your intuitions, treat them tenderly and cultivate the conditions that enable them to flourish.

The process of becoming a teacher of gifted children is indeed an exciting and rewarding adventure.

References

Anderson, J. E. "The Nature of Abilities." In E. P. Torrance (Ed.) *Talent and Education*. Minneapolis: University of Minnesota Press, 1960, pp. 9–13.

Anderson, K. E. (ed.). *Research on the Academically Talented Student*. Washington, D.C.: National Education Association, 1961.

Applegate, Mauree. *Easy in English*. Evanston: Harper and Row, 1962.

Barron, F. "Originality in Relation to Personality and Intellect." *Journal of Personality*, 25 (1957), 730–42.

——— "Diffusion, Integration, and Enduring Attention in the Creative Process." In R. W. White (ed.). *The Study of Lives*. New York: Atherton, 1963, pp. 234–49.

Bayley, Nancy. "Mental Growth in Young Children." In *Yearbook of the National Society for the Study of Education*, 39(11) (1940), 11–47.

Binet, A. *Les Idées Modernes sur les Enfants*. Paris, Flamarion, 1909.

Bloom, B. S. "Some Effects of Cultural, Social, and Educational Conditions on Creativity." In C. W. Taylor (ed.). *The Second (1957) University of Utah Research Conference on the Identification of Creative Scientific Talent*. Salt Lake City: University of Utah Press, 1958, pp. 55–65.

Bruner, J. S. *The Process of Education*. Cambridge: Harvard University Press, 1960.

Burkhart, R. C. *Spontaneous and Deliberate Ways of Learning*. Scranton: International Textbook Company, 1962.

Burt, C. "The Inheritance of Mental Ability." *American Psychologist*, 13 (1958), 1–15.

Ciardi, J. *I Met a Man*. Cambridge: Pathways of Sound, Inc., 1962.

Cunnington, B. F., Pearl Buckland, and R. G. Peterson. *Giovanni and the Giant*. Minneapolis: Bureau of Educational Research, University of Minnesota, 1962.

——— R. E. Myers, Pearl Buckland, and R. G. Peterson. *Eyes at Their Fingertips*. Minneapolis: Bureau of Educational Research, University of Minnesota, 1962.

93

de Groot, A. D. "The Effects of War upon the Intelligence of Youth." *Journal of Abnormal and Social Psychology*, **43** (1948), 311–17.

——. "War and Intelligence of Youth." *Journal of Abnormal and Social Psychology*, **46** (1951), 596–7.

Dinkmeyer, D., and R. Dreikurs. *Encouraging Children to Learn*. Englewood Cliffs, N.J.: Prentice-Hall, 1963.

Drews, Elizabeth M. "A Critical Evaluation of Approaches to the Identification of Gifted Students." In A. Traxler (ed.). *Measurement and Evaluation in Today's Schools*. Washington, D.C.: American Council on Education, 1961, pp. 47–51. (a)

+ ——. "Recent Findings About Gifted Adolescents." In E. P. Torrance (ed.) *New Educational Ideas: Third Minnesota Conference on Gifted Children*. Minneapolis: Center for Continuation Study, University of Minnesota, 1961. (b)

Durrell, D. "Pupil Team Learning: Effects on Team Size on Retention of Knowledge." Paper presented at Annual Meeting of the American Educational Research Association, Chicago, February 24, 1961.

——, and J. R. Chambers. "Research in Thinking Abilities Related to Reading." *Reading Teacher*, **12** (1958), 89–91.

+ Ferbee, June D. "Learning Through Creative Expression." *Elementary English*, **27** (1950), 73–8.

+ Fleigler, L. A. (ed.). *Curriculum Planning for the Gifted*. Englewood Cliffs, N.J.: Prentice-Hall, 1961.

Frankel, E. "The Gifted Academic Underachiever." *Science Teacher*, **28** (1961), 49–51.

Fritz, R. L. "An Evaluation of Scholastic Achievement of Students Attending Half-Day Sessions in the Seventh Grade." Unpublished M.A. research paper, University of Minnesota, August 1958.

+ Gallagher, J. J. *Analysis of Research on the Education of Gifted Children*. Springfield, Ill.: Office of the Superintendent of Public Instruction, 1960.

——. *Teaching the Gifted Child*. Boston: Allyn & Bacon, 1964.

+ Getzels, J. W., and Jackson, P. W. *Creativity and Intelligence*. New York: Wiley, 1962.

Goertzel, V., and Mildred George Goertzel. *Cradles of Eminence*. Boston: Little, Brown, 1962.

+ Gordon, W. J. J. *Synectics: The Development of Creative Capacity*. New York: Harper & Row, 1961.

Gowan, J. C. "Recent Research on the Education of Gifted Children." *Psychological Newsletter*, **9** (March 1958), 140–4.

Guilford, J. P. "Structure of Intellect." *Psychological Bulletin*, **53** (1956), 267–93.

——. "Three Faces of Intellect." *American Psychologist*, **14** (1959), 469–79. (a)

—— *Personality*. New York: McGraw-Hill, 1959. (b)

——. "Factorial Angles to Psychology." *Psychological Review*, **68** (1961), 1–20.

———. "What to Do About Creativity in Education." In *Conference Proceedings of the Educational Testing Service.* Los Angeles: Educational Testing Service, 1962. (a)

———. "Factors That Aid and Hinder Creativity." *Teachers College Record,* **63** (1962), 380–92. (b)

———, and R. Hoepfner. *Current Structure-of-Intellect Factors and Suggested Tests.* Los Angeles: University of Southern California, 1963.

Heathers, G. "The Dual-Progress Plan." *Educational Leadership,* **18** (1960), 76–8, 121.

Heys, F., Jr. "The Theme-a-Week Assumption: A Report of An Experiment." *English Journal,* **51** (1962), 320–2.

Hoch, O. "Improving the Present Status of the Creative Student." *High School Journal,* **46** (1962), 14–22.

Honzik, Marjorie P., Jean W. Macfarlane, and L. Allen. "The Stability of Mental Test Performance Between Two and Eighteen Years." *Journal of Experimental Education,* **4** (1948), 309–24.

Hunt, J. McV. *Intelligence and Experience.* New York: Ronald, 1961.

Hutchinson, W. L. *Creative and Productive Thinking in the Classroom.* Doctoral dissertation, University of Utah, Salt Lake City, Utah, 1961.

Hyman, R. "On Prior Information and Creativity." *Psychological Reports,* **9** (1961), 151–61.

Lorge, I. "Schooling Makes a Difference." *Teachers College Record,* **46** (1945), 483–92.

McConnell, T. R. "Discovery vs. Authoritative Identification in the Learning of Children." *University of Iowa Studies in Education,* **9(5)** 1934, 13–62.

McKeachie, W. J. "Motivating Students' Interest." In R. M. Cooper (ed.). *The Two Ends of the Log.* Minneapolis: University of Minnesota Press, 1958, pp. 36–9.

MacKinnon, D. W. (ed.). *The Creative Person.* Berkeley: University of California, University Extension, 1961.

Mead, Margaret. *The School in American Culture.* Cambridge: Harvard University Press, 1955.

Moore, O. K. "Orthographic Symbols and the Pre-School Child—A New Approach." In E. P. Torrance (ed.). *New Educational Ideas: Third Minnesota Conference on Gifted Children.* Minneapolis: Center for Continuation Study, University of Minnesota, 1961, pp. 91–101.

Munari, B. *Who's There? Open the Door.* New York: World, 1957.

———. *The Elephant's Wish.* New York: World, 1959. (a)

———. *The Birthday Present.* New York: World, 1959. (b)

Newman, H. H., F. N. Freeman, and K. J. Holzinger. *Twins: A Study of Heredity and Environment.* Chicago: University of Chicago Press, 1937.

Ojemann, R. H. "Research in Planned Learning Programs and the Science of Behavior." *Journal of Educational Research,* **42** (1948), 96–104.

Ojemann, R. H., and Karen Pritchett. "Piaget and the Role of Guided Experiences in Human Development." *Perceptual and Motor Skills,* **17** (1963), 927–39.

Ornstein, J. "New Recruits for Science." *Parent's Magazine,* **36(42)** (February 1961), 101–103.

Passow, A. H. "Enrichment of Education for the Gifted." In N. B. Henry (ed.). *Education for the Gifted* (Fifty-seventh Yearbook, National Society for the Study of Education). Chicago: University of Chicago Press, 1958, pp. 193–221.

Piaget, J. *The Psychology of Intelligence.* London: Routledge and Kegan Paul, 1951.

–––. *Language and Thought of the Child.* New York: Meridian, 1955.

Pressey, S. L. "The Most Misunderstood Concept, Acceleration." *School and Society,* **79** (1954), 59–60.

Reynolds, M. C. "Acceleration." In E. P. Torrance (ed.). *Talent and Education.* Minneapolis: University of Minnesota Press, 1960. pp. 106–25.

Riessman, F. *The Culturally Deprived Child.* New York: Harper & Row, 1962.

Roe, Anne. *The Making of a Scientist.* New York: Dodd, Mead, 1952.

–––. "Crucial Life Experiences in the Development of Scientists." In E. P. Torrance (ed.). *Education and Talent.* Minneapolis: University of Minnesota, 1960, pp. 66–77.

–––. "Personal Problems and Science." In C. W. Taylor and F. Barron (eds.). *Scientific Creativity: Its Recognition and Development.* New York: Wiley, 1963, pp. 132–8.

Rosenbloom, P. C. (ed.). *Modern Viewpoints in the Curriculum.* New York: McGraw-Hill, 1964.

Rossman, J. *The Psychology of the Inventor.* Washington, D.C.: Inventors Publishing Company, 1931.

Shane, H. G. "Grouping in the Elementary School." *Phi Delta Kappan,* **40** (1960), 313–18.

Shotka, Josephine. "Creative Reading." *Education,* **82** (1961), 26–8.

Spencer, L. M. "Oklahoma Identifies Its Talented Youth." In *The Oklahoma Science Education Story.* New York: Thomas Alva Edison Foundation, 1957, pp. 9–1.

Spitz, R. A. "Hospitalism: An Inquiry into the Genesis of Psychiatric Conditions in Early Childhood." *Psychoanalytic Studies of the Child,* **1** (1945), 53–74.

–––. "Hospitalism: A Follow-up Report." *Psychoanalytic Studies of the Child,* **2** (1946), 113–17.

Standing, E. M. *Maria Montessori: Her Life and Work.* New York: Mentor-Omega Books, 1962.

Stolurow, L. M. "Social Impact of Programmed Instruction: Aptitudes and Abilities Revisited." Paper presented at the Annual Convention of the American Psychological Association, St. Louis, Missouri, September 3, 1962.

Suchman, J. R. "Inquiry Training: Building Skills for Autonomous Discovery." *Merrill-Palmer Quarterly,* **7** (1961), 147–70.

Taylor, C. W. "Who Are the Exceptionally Creative?" *Exceptional Children,* **28** (1962), 421–31.

—— (ed.). *Creativity: Progress and Potential.* New York: McGraw-Hill, 1964. (a)

Taylor, C. W. "Developing Creative Characteristics." *The Instructor,* **73**(9) (May 1964), 5, 99–100. (b)

——. "Developing Creative Thinking." *The Instructor,* **73**(8) (April 1964), 7, 71–2. (c)

Terman, L. M. "The Discovery and Encouragement of Exceptional Talent." *American Psychologist,* **9** (1954), 221–30.

+Torrance, E. P. (ed.). *Talent and Education.* Minneapolis: University of Minnesota Press, 1960.

——. "Curriculum Frontiers for the Elementary Gifted Pupil: Flying Monkeys and Silent Lions." *Exceptional Children,* **28** (1961), 119–27.

——. *Guiding Creative Talent.* Englewood Cliffs, N.J.: Prentice-Hall, 1962. (a)

——. "Cultural Discontinuities and the Development of Originality of Thinking." *Exceptional Children,* **29** (1962), 2–13. (b)

——. *Education and the Creative Potential.* Minneapolis: University of Minnesota Press, 1963. (a)

——. "The Creative Personality and the Ideal Pupil." *Teachers College Record,* **65** (1963), 220–6.

——. *Role of Evaluation in Creative Thinking.* (Cooperative Research Project No. 725.) Minneapolis: Bureau of Educational Research, University of Minnesota, 1964. (a)

——. "Education and Creativity." In C. W. Taylor (ed.). *Creativity: Progress and Potential.* New York: McGraw-Hill, 1964, pp. 129–54. (b)

——, and Kevser Arsan. "Experimental Studies of Homogeneous and Heterogeneous Groups for Creative Scientific Tasks." In W. W. Charters, Jr. and N. L. Gage (eds.). *Readings in the Social Psychology of Education.* Boston: Allyn and Bacon, 1963. pp. 133–40.

——, and J. A. Harmon. "Effects of Memory, Evaluative, and Creative Reading Sets on Test Performance." *Journal of Educational Psychology,* **52** (1961), 207–14.

——, and R. E. Myers. "Teaching Gifted Elementary Pupils Research Concepts and Skills." *Gifted Child Quarterly,* **6** (1962), 1–16. (a)

—— and Myers, R. E. *Teaching Gifted Elementary Pupils How to Do Research.* Minneapolis: Perceptive Publishing Company, 1962. (b)

Vernon, P. E. "Changes in Abilities from 14 to 20 Years." *Advanced Science*, **5** (1948), 138.

Ward, V. S. (chmn.). *The Gifted Student: A Manual for Program Improvement*. Atlanta: Southern Regional Education Board, 1962.

Whyte, W. H., Jr. *The Organization Man*. Garden City, N.Y.: Doubleday Anchor Books, 1957.

Witty, P. A. (ed.). *The Gifted Child*. Boston: Heath, 1951.

Yamamoto, K. "Threshold of Intelligence in Academic Achievement of Highly Creative Students." *Journal of Experimental Education*, **32** (1964), 401–5.

Appendix A

What Kind of Persons Do You Want the Children You Teach to Become?

What kind of persons would you like the children you teach to become? Please try to describe the kind of persons you would like for your pupils to become by using the checklist of characteristics on this sheet. Check each of the characteristics you think is generally desirable and should be encouraged. Then double check the characteristics you consider most important and should be encouraged above all others. Draw a line through those characteristics you consider undesirable and usually discourage or punish.

————Adventurous
————Affectionate
————Altruistic
————Always asking questions
————Attempts difficult jobs
————A self-starter
————A good guesser
————Bashful
————Becomes preoccupied with tasks
————Conforming
————Considerate of others
————Courageous in convictions
————Courteous
————Competitive
————Critical of others
————Curious
————Desires to excel
————Determination
————Domineering
————Disturbs procedures or
     organization
————Does work on time
————Emotional
————Emotionally sensitive
————Energetic
————Fault-finding
————Haughty and self-satisfied
————Healthy
————Independent in judgment
————Independent in thinking
————Industrious
————Likes to work alone
————Intuitive

————Never bored
————Negativistic
————Obedient
————Persistent
————Popular, well liked by peers
————Prefers complex tasks
————Physically strong
————Quiet
————Receptive to ideas of others
————Regresses occasionally
     (playful, childish)
————Reserved
————Remembers well
————Self-confident
————Self-assertive
————Self-sufficient
————Sense of humor
————Sense of beauty
————Sincere
————Spirited in disagreement
————Strives for distant goals
————Stubborn
————Timid
————Thorough
————Talkative
————Unsophisticated
————Unwilling to accept things
     on mere say-so
————Versatile
————Visionary
————Willing to take risks
————Willing to accept judgments
     of authorities

Appendix B

HOW DID YOU GROW?

Name: _____ Grade: _____

Age: ___ Teacher: _____ School: _____

What kind of work do you want to do when you grow up? _____

In order to get an accurate picture of how you grew, we would have to take some kind of measurement at regular intervals of some kind—every year, every six months, every month, and the like. Even though careful records have not been taken, it is frequently possible to use various sources of information to construct a fairly good picture of various aspects of your growth. Today, I would like you to make as good guesses as you can about eight different aspects of your growth from the first through sixth grade. Between now and tomorrow I want you to try in as many ways as you can to correct your guesses and construct as accurate a picture as you can about the way you have grown. You can use your own ingenuity in checking your guesses.

In some characteristics your growth has been smooth and uninterrupted. In others your growth has been up and down. In still others you have grown a while, stood still, and then grown very rapidly. In the graph at the left we have a typical picture of the way most boys and girls grow in weight. At the right is a graph of the way most boys and girls grow in their ability to ask questions. On the sheets which follow, you will be asked to draw pictures like this of the way you have grown.

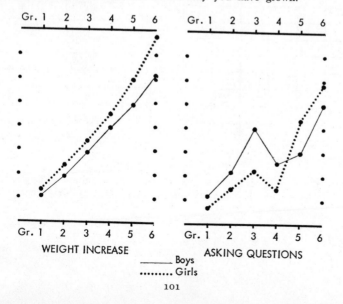

WEIGHT INCREASE   ASKING QUESTIONS

_____ Boys
.... Girls

HOW DID YOU GROW?

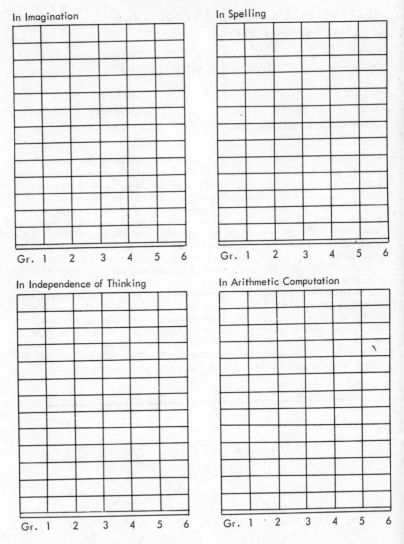

In Imagination

In Spelling

Gr. 1   2   3   4   5   6

In Independence of Thinking

In Arithmetic Computation

Gr. 1   2   3   4   5   6

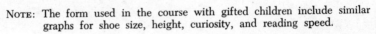

NOTE: The form used in the course with gifted children include similar graphs for shoe size, height, curiosity, and reading speed.